Bake Me
a Cake as
Fast as
You Can

To my very own Team GB:

Edward for being my motivator and constant source of encouragement. For his way with words and for loving my cakes, even when he was made to eat them for breakfast, lunch and supper! Thomas for his unfaltering praise and calming reassurance, for loving my baking adventures, and for providing much-needed distraction in bouncing on the trampoline and going for muddy walks. Eleanor for her passion for baking, her expert assistance, her need for a constant supply of cakes for fairy tea parties with friends, and for her creativity and our shared love of decorating. My very own 'apple tree fairy'. And little Henry, cake in one hand, muslin in the other, who has been lulled to sleep by mixers, kept me company in the kitchen and, being too little to talk, conveyed cake happiness through his smiling face.

Bake Me a Cake as Fast as You Can

Over 100 super easy, delicious & quick recipes

Miranda Gore Browne

EBURY
PRESS

10 9 8 7 6 5 4 3 2 1

Published in 2014 by Ebury Press, an imprint of Ebury Publishing

A Random House Group Company

Text © Miranda Gore Browne 2014
Photography by Rosie Barnett © Ebury Press 2014

The Random House Group Limited Reg. No. 954009

Addresses for companies within the Random House Group can be found at www.randomhouse.co.uk

A CIP catalogue record for this book is available from the British Library

The Random House Group Limited supports the Forest Stewardship Council® (FSC®), the leading international forest-certification organisation. Our books carrying the FSC label are printed on FSC®-certified paper. FSC is the only forest-certification scheme supported by the leading environmental organisations, including Greenpeace. Our paper procurement policy can be found at www.randomhouse.co.uk/environment

To buy books by your favourite authors and register for offers visit www.randomhouse.co.uk

Design: Lucy Stephens
Photography: Rosie Barnett
Food stylist: Annie Rigg
Prop stylist: Sarah Moore

Colour origination by Altaimage, London
Printed and bound in China by C&C Offset Printing Co., Ltd

ISBN 9780091945114

CONTENTS

INTRODUCTION

I've baked cakes since I was very little. Some of my happiest memories are of standing on a chair at the worktop making cakes and, of course, licking the bowl. Indeed, many of my childhood memories are associated with cake – the tins of cake we took on holidays to the Lake District and enjoyed on picnics wearing our 'hill walking jumpers', the comforting taste of little chocolate buns we loved eating still warm, the cakes we made after school, and my mother decorating our much-loved family fruit cake with 'rough snow' royal icing every Christmas Eve.

I'm always baking something, however busy I am working, looking after our three children, running a home and keeping up with other commitments. When I worked long hours in my career at M&S I found baking cakes an escape and found great relaxation returning from a work trip to the comfort of my kitchen to make a cake. Even when we go on holiday I bake cakes, as that is what family time together is all about for me.

Bake Me a Cake as Fast as You Can isn't just about making cakes in a hurry. It's also about real baking for real lives. Most people say they just don't have the time to bake a cake. I hope this book will show you that you do. I want to give you the confidence to make delicious homemade cakes in a jiffy, while also demystifying the cake baking process.

Some of the recipes in this book really are super quick, while others will help you to make a special cake in much less time than you thought it would take. Cakes can be made when you are dashing in from work, rushing back from the school run, or at the last minute before friends arrive. It's not all about racing against the clock but more about believing you can make cakes even if time is short. The best thing about a homemade cake is that it doesn't matter if it's not perfect to look at (although it may well be!); it will taste delicious, and everyone will be thrilled you made it.

Cakes don't need to be baked only at times set aside at the weekend. I don't think they should require planning or always use special ingredients. One of the tests I have applied to many of these recipes is 'can I make this cake now while I juggle everything else?'. As I write and test recipes, I always look around my kitchen and think about whether people will have particular ingredients in their cupboards. What's ideal about making homemade cakes is that they require just a few simple ingredients, and it's so much faster and easier to get baking if you have the right things available.

Friends and family tell me they want trusted, tested recipes that they can whip up confidently. The recipes in this book range from super-speedy loaf cakes you can make in five minutes to pretty decorated cakes for special occasions that can be whizzed together far faster than you thought possible. It is often a great deal quicker to bake a cake than to go to the shops to buy one.

I make all the cakes in the book regularly in my basic family kitchen, usually with life rushing by around me, and often with many interruptions. In fact the frenzy of family life was at its height when I was writing and testing these recipes. My kitchen (and most of my house) was being dismantled around me while we underwent a major building project! On many occasions the builders had to switch off our power or water or remove a part of the kitchen.

I bake and test everything myself, and it is my family and friends who taste, taste and taste again and tell me what they think. Children tend to be the most honest of testers, and mine do not hold back! The recipes, here, have been tested by some of those friends and family members, a number of whom have confronted long-held fears of baking, to check that the recipes really are as quick and easy as I say they are.

Traybakes are great because they make lots of pieces of cake very quickly. I have snuck a few into this book that have secret middles (you bake the filling in the cake to save time).

I often hear myself saying 'I'll bring pudding' to help out when friends invite us for dinner. I try to be fairly organised, but there are occasions when Saturdays have run away with me and I need to bake the promised cake at the last minute. My pudding cakes are well tested, and are usually devoured at a great rate of knots. Hopefully these cakes will be useful helpers for your puddings at home. I have included some tips for pudding kits to get them safely to their destination too.

Baking really can be super quick. Some of the loaf cakes take less than five minutes to mix up and may leave you wondering why you used to go to the supermarket to buy fruit loaf or some teatime treats.

There are some very simple cakes in the little cakes and loaf cakes chapters which I would point any novice baker (young or old) towards if they are looking for the simplest recipes with the quickest results. All of these cakes are easy to make.

Whether you are making fruit loaves or little iced buns that don't require rising or proving, or 'puddle' cakes that don't need icing or filling, I hope this book will help you to bake wonderful cakes quickly and simply.

Some of the recipes benefit from an electric hand whisk, or from a food processor for finely grinding, but there are many others that can be made by hand with nothing more than a bowl and a wooden spoon. I am unlikely to get sugar thermometers or other technical equipment out on an average day. I have tried, wherever possible, to find alternatives to complicated methods and unusual ingredients.

I have included some tips for variations on recipes. If a recipe works as well for cupcakes as for big cakes, I think it is useful for you to know. I also love to use the same recipe, but to decorate it in different ways. I will share some of my favourites with you throughout the book.

I thought long and hard about whether to include a children's chapter. In the end, I decided not to do so. Who am I to assume which of these cakes a child might want or be able to make? I am constantly delighted by the ability of children to bake really well, and by their creativity and enthusiasm for new recipes and flavours. I hope you might bake lots of these cakes with children, and, who knows, you might soon even have children bake some for you!

I am passionate about encouraging people to believe they can make any cake they choose. Perhaps I am rather evangelical about getting everyone baking, however short of time they are. But there is always time to make a cake!

Happy cake baking!

Love, Miranda xx

SPEEDY TIPS

Cake tin liners save so much time. It is worth buying them in a few tin sizes. They are much quicker than lining tins with baking paper, and allow you to lift cakes straight out in their liners, avoiding spilling crumbs all over the counter! They also make cakes easier to transport.

Planning ahead can really speed things up. Five minutes spent checking ingredients, ensuring butter is in a warm place to soften, and perhaps weighing a few things; quickly popping chocolate and cream into a bowl over a pan of simmering water then leaving the resulting delicious ganache to cool (this is often something I can be found doing early in the morning whilst getting breakfast ready).

A well-stocked kitchen will help too. I try to always have the following ingredients in my kitchen.

In the cupboard: lemon curd, chocolate spread, jams, pesto, runny honey, dulce de leche; caramel, syrup, treacle; sultanas, raisins, dried apricots and figs, nuts, seeds; chocolate (dark 70% cocoa solids as well as white and milk chocolate) in bars and chocolate chips or chunks plus sweets, flakes, crunchie bars; spices, including cinnamon, ginger, vanilla pods and extract; dark brown soft sugar, light brown soft sugar, caster sugar, granulated sugar and icing sugar; plain flour, self-raising flour, baking powder, bicarbonate of soda, cocoa powder, oats and sea salt.

In the fridge: unsalted butter (have a few packs in the freezer as well), large eggs, double cream, cheese, bananas, seasonal fruit, milk, plain yoghurt.

In the freezer: mixed berries, raspberries and unsalted butter.

GIVING CAKES AS PRESENTS

Bake a double batch and give one to a friend.

Personalise cakes with an iced initial or sugar flowers to make a name. Sugar flowers can make simple cakes extra special – it is useful to have a supply of these in your kitchen.

Keep a stock of cellophane bags and cake boxes for wrapping cakes. Pretty ribbons can be tied round simple cakes or round the packaging.

Edible flowers make the prettiest decorations, and a few tiny pansies, primroses or nasturtiums are a lovely touch. To make crystallised flowers, stretch baking paper over a cake tin and tie with string then make small holes in the paper ready for the flower stems. Use a balloon whisk to whisk one egg white until frothy. Brush the egg white over the flower petals with a small paintbrush then gently use a spoon to sprinkle over the caster sugar. Push the stem of each flower through a hole in the prepared paper then leave to dry overnight in a warm place.

FREEZING CAKES

Lots of the cakes freeze really well, and I often make a double batch and pop one in the freezer. When you take cakes out of the freezer it is best to defrost them at room temperature. Once a cake is defrosted, a useful tip is to pop it in the microwave on the defrost setting for about two minutes. This makes the cake springy and moist and tasting as if you have just made it!

BIG CAKES

BLACKBERRY CAKE

This is a lovely, simple recipe for blackberry cake, and a good way to use up all the blackberries you pick. It's a great cake to enjoy with a cup of tea, or it can be smartened up into a comforting pudding for an autumnal Sunday lunch or supper – just add a blob of mascarpone (or clotted cream) and a generous sift of icing sugar! It also freezes well so, if you've been a proficient picker, you can make lots of cakes to put in the freezer; that way you can enjoy your blackberries all year round.

SERVES 6–8	MAKING TIME	BAKING TIME
	10-15 minutes	1 hour

275 g blackberries (don't worry if you have less), unwashed

150 g unsalted butter

3 large eggs

150 g caster sugar (or vanilla sugar), plus extra for sprinkling

2 tbsp demerara sugar

1 tsp vanilla essence, or seeds from 1 vanilla pod

250 g plain flour

1½ tsp baking powder

125 ml semi-skimmed milk

1 Preheat the oven to 180°C (350°F/Gas 4). Line a 23-cm springform cake tin that is at least 6 cm deep with a cake tin liner – these are fantastic as this is quite a runny batter. Alternatively use non-stick baking paper.

2 Check through the blackberries for dirt and brush off any dirt with a piece of kitchen towel (washing them will add water to the mix), and put to one side. Melt the butter, and set aside.

3 Put the eggs, sugars and vanilla into the bowl of an electric mixer fitted with a balloon whisk attachment and whisk until pale and fluffy; alternatively use a hand-held electric mixer.

4 Sift in the flour and baking powder, and mix until incorporated. Pour the melted butter and milk into the mix, and whisk again.

5 Sprinkle a handful of the blackberries into the bottom of the prepared tin. Pour about half of the cake mix over the top of the blackberries. Sprinkle half of the remaining blackberries over the cake mix, then add the remaining cake mix. Finally sprinkle the remaining blackberries over the top and sprinkle with caster sugar (or vanilla sugar if you have some).

6 Put the cake tin on a baking sheet (to catch spillages) and bake in the preheated oven for about 1 hour, or until the cake is golden on top and a skewer comes out clean.

7 Remove from the oven and leave to cool before taking out of the tin.

BRIGHTON SPONGE

My mother-in-law used to make this for coffee mornings in the 1970s. It's a delicious almond cake with a hidden layer of baked jam. I hope she won't mind me saying it rather reminds me of the kind of cake Margot might have served in *The Good Life*.

SERVES 6	MAKING TIME	BAKING TIME
	10–15 minutes	30 minutes

170 g self-raising flour

85 g caster sugar, plus extra for sprinkling

85 g unsalted butter

1 large egg

2 tsp almond extract

4–5 tbsp strawberry or raspberry jam

blanched whole almonds, to decorate

1 Preheat the oven to 180°C (350°F/Gas 4) and line an 18-cm round sandwich cake tin with a cake tin liner or use non-stick baking paper.

2 Mix together the flour and sugar in a bowl and then rub in the butter with your fingertips; alternatively whizz in a food processor.

3 Beat the egg and almond extract together with a fork, then add to the butter, sugar and flour mixture, mixing well with a fork or whizzing again in the food processor. The mixture should come together as a sticky ball of dough.

4 Split into two rough balls. Press one ball into the base of the prepared tin and flatten (you may need to dip a fork in some flour to press it down as it's rather sticky).

5 Spread with the jam and press the remaining dough on top (again dipping a fork in flour helps to do this neatly).

6 Press the almonds around the edge of the cake, pushing them into the surface with your fingers.

7 Bake in the preheated oven for 30 minutes until the cake is golden and shrinking away from the sides of the tin. Remove from the oven and sprinkle with caster sugar. Leave to cool in the tin before slicing and serving.

Miranda's variation

Replace the almond extract with the zest of 1 lemon and 2 teaspoons of lemon juice. Keep the raspberry jam or replace with lemon curd.

REALLY GOOD CHERRY CAKE

Sometimes the simplest things taste the best. My mother used to make this cake all the time when we were little, and every time I bake it I remember why. I'm surprised any cherries ever found their way into the cake, given my reputation for stealing them from the cupboard!

SERVES 6–8	MAKING TIME 10 minutes	BAKING TIME 45 minutes

175 g unsalted butter, softened

175 g caster sugar, plus 2 tbsp for sprinkling

3 large eggs

250 g self-raising flour

2–3 tbsp semi-skimmed milk

1 tsp vanilla extract

200 g glacé cherries, halved

1 Preheat the oven to 180°C (350°F/Gas 4) and line a 20-cm round cake tin with a cake tin liner or non-stick baking paper.

2 Cream together the butter and sugar. Add the eggs and beat well to combine.

3 Add the flour, milk and vanilla and mix gently to combine. Fold in the halved cherries with a spoon.

4 Spoon the mixture into the prepared tin and smooth the top with a palette knife. Sprinkle some caster sugar on top then bake the cake in the preheated oven for about 45 minutes, or until golden and springy to the touch.

This can also be made in a 20 x 30-cm tray bake tin, in which case reduce the cooking time to 25–30 minutes.

FROSTED RASPBERRY AND REDCURRANT CAKE

A simple cake, baked with the freshest of summer berries. The frosty white topping and some extra fruit are the only adornments it requires. This makes one 20-cm round cake to two 2-lb loaf cakes.

SERVES 6–8

MAKING TIME
10–15 minutes

BAKING TIME
35 minutes

---

200 g unsalted butter, softened

225 g caster sugar

1 tsp vanilla extract

300 g self-raising flour

2 tsp baking powder

4 large eggs

6 tbsp semi-skimmed milk

150 g raspberries, picked clean but unwashed

150 g redcurrants, picked clean but unwashed

For the topping

1 large egg white

110 g icing sugar

1 tsp lemon juice

Extra raspberries and redcurrants to decorate (optional)

1 Preheat the oven to 180°C (350°F/Gas 4) and line a deep 20-cm round cake tin (or two 2-lb loaf tins) with non-stick baking paper.

2 Put all the ingredients for the cake, except the fruit, into the bowl of an electric mixer and mix well. Gently fold in the fruit with a metal spoon.

3 Spoon the mixture into the prepared tin (or tins) and bake in the preheated oven for about 30 minutes, or until the cake is golden on top and a skewer comes out clean.

4 To make the topping whisk the egg white with a balloon whisk until frothy, then whisk in the icing sugar and lemon juice. Brush on top of the cake as soon as it comes out of the oven. Return to the oven for a further 5 minutes (this bakes the pretty frosting), then remove from the oven and leave to cool in the tin. Decorate with some extra raspberries redcurrants and lightly dust with icing sugar, if you like.

SUMMERY RHUBARB CAKE

Unbelievably easy to make, this light, orange-scented cake is made with rhubarb chopped straight from the garden. The orange works its magic and intensifies the rhubarb flavour, and a simple sprinkling of sugar on top is the only finishing touch. Lovely with a cup of tea, but also perfect with clotted cream as an informal summery pudding.

SERVES 6–8	MAKING TIME	BAKING TIME
	10–15 minutes	40 minutes

225 g rhubarb

200 g unsalted butter, softened

160 g caster sugar, plus extra for sprinkling

grated zest and juice of 1 orange (about 2–3 tbsp juice)

3 large eggs, lightly beaten

225 g self-raising flour

40 g granulated sugar

1 Preheat the oven to 180°C (350°F/Gas 4) and line a 20-cm round springform cake tin with a cake tin liner or non-stick baking paper.

2 Chop the rhubarb into 1-2cm pieces and put to one side; if you washed it, dry with a clean tea towel before chopping.

3 Cream together the butter and caster sugar with the orange zest on a high speed until pale and fluffy. Add the eggs and beat again at a high speed.

4 Gently mix in the flour and orange juice and then fold in two-thirds of the rhubarb.

5 Scrape into the prepared tin. Sprinkle the granulated sugar over the remaining rhubarb then spread on top of the cake.

6 Bake in the preheated oven for about 40 minutes, until pale golden and firm yet springy to the touch. Remove from the oven and sprinkle with caster sugar before serving.

GRINDELWALD MUESLI CAKE

Oats, brown sugar and milk baked to create a dense and nourishing Swiss-style muesli cake – perfect on a picnic or with thick yoghurt and fruit for brunch. There is a spot by a mountain stream, above the town of Grindelwald in the Swiss Alps, where my husband spent his childhood summer holidays. He still describes it as his favourite place on earth. And this cake is a slice of that place.

SERVES 8	MAKING TIME	BAKING TIME
	10 minutes (including standing time)	45 minutes

175 g muesli

150 ml semi-skimmed milk

175 g self-raising flour

175 g demerara sugar, plus extra for sprinkling

175 g chilled unsalted butter, cut into cubes

3 large eggs, beaten

1 Preheat the oven to 180°C (350°F/Gas 4) and line the base of a 23-cm round loose-bottomed cake tin with a cake tin liner; alternatively lightly grease the sides and use non-stick baking paper.

2 Put the muesli into a bowl and pour over the milk; leave to stand while you get on with the rest of the recipe.

3 Put the flour and sugar into a bowl and stir together, then rub in the butter with your fingertips. Add the eggs and the milky muesli and beat well with a wooden spoon.

4 Scrape into the prepared tin, level and smooth. Sprinkle over a little extra sugar and bake in the preheated oven for about 45 minutes, until golden brown and coming away from the sides of the tin. Leave to cool in the tin, although the cake is also delicious eaten while still warm.

HOT CROSS BUN CAKE

No resting, no proving, no yeast! This is a fast and tasty alternative to hot cross buns that would make a lovely addition to an Easter tea party – it is also super-quick to make.

SERVES 8	MAKING TIME	BAKING TIME
	15 minutes	35 minutes

170 g self-raising flour

170 g wholemeal plain flour (or use 340 g self-raising flour and omit the baking powder)

1 tsp baking powder

½ tsp salt

85 g caster sugar

1 tsp nutmeg

1 tsp mixed spice

2 tsp grated orange zest

2 tsp grated lemon zest

140 g sultanas

1 eating apple, peeled, cored and finely chopped

2 large eggs

265 ml semi-skimmed milk

55 g unsalted butter, melted

2 tbsp apricot jam, to glaze

icing sugar, to dust the cross

1 Preheat the oven to 180°C (350°F/Gas 4) and line a 20-cm round cake tin with a cake tin liner or non-stick baking paper.

2 Put the flours, baking powder, salt, sugar, spices, zest, sultanas and apple into a large bowl and mix to combine.

3 Break the eggs into a jug, add the milk and mix well with a fork then add the melted butter.

4 Pour the milk mixture on to the dry ingredients and mix well with a wooden spoon. Scrape into the prepared tin and bake in the preheated oven for 35 minutes, or until golden and firm yet springy to the touch.

5 As soon as the cake comes out of the oven, spoon the apricot jam over the top. Leave to cool a little then fold a piece of baking paper into four and cut along the folds to make a cross in the paper. Lay across the top of the cake, dust with icing sugar then remove the paper to reveal the cross.

Miranda's variation

To make individual cakes, spoon the mixture into muffin tins lined with paper cases (this quantity will make 18 buns). Reduce the baking time to 15–20 minutes.

SPEEDY FRUIT CAKE

A delectable fruit cake that can be made with storecupboard ingredients. The walnuts add a homely depth to the flavour and the ground almonds ensure it keeps well. This is a great cake to enjoy with coffee.

SERVES 8	MAKING TIME	BAKING TIME
	15 minutes	2 hours (or 40–45 minutes if made as a tray bake)

170 g unsalted butter, softened

170 g soft brown sugar

3 large eggs

285 g plain flour

1 tsp baking powder

450 g dried fruit (I use whatever I have in – usually sultanas and currants)

60 g ground almonds

1 tsp grated lemon zest

30 g walnut halves, crushed roughly in your hands

pinch of salt

1 tbsp semi-skimmed milk

50 g flaked almonds (optional)

1 Preheat the oven to 170°C (325°F/Gas 3). Line a deep 20-cm cake tin with a cake tin liner or non-stick baking paper; alternatively this can be made in a 20 x 30-cm tray bake tin.

2 Cream together the butter and sugar and then beat in the eggs.

3 Mix in all the remaining ingredients, except the flaked almonds, and spoon into the prepared tin. Scatter the flaked almonds, if using, on to the top.

4 Cover with foil and bake in the preheated oven for about 1½ hours. Remove the foil and return to the oven for a further 25–30 minutes. Check whether the cake is done by inserting a skewer or sharp knife into the centre; it should come out clean.

FIGGY HAZELNUT CAKE

Baked with figs, warming cinnamon and toasted hazelnuts, and topped with crunchy demerara, this cake is wonderful with mugs of coffee and lots of good conversation.

SERVES 8

MAKING TIME
10–15 minutes

BAKING TIME
25–30 minutes

125 g unsalted butter

125 g caster sugar

3 large eggs

80 g ground almonds

50 g self-raising flour

pinch of salt

1 tbsp semi-skimmed milk

125 g dried figs, diced into small pieces

½ tsp ground cinnamon

150 g toasted hazelnuts, roughly chopped

1 tbsp demerara sugar, for sprinkling

1 Preheat the oven to 180°C (350°F/Gas 4). Line a 23-cm round shallow cake tin with non-stick baking paper or use a cake tin liner.

2 Cream together the butter and caster sugar then beat in the eggs.

3 Gently mix in the almonds, flour, salt and milk and then fold in the figs, cinnamon and 125g of the hazelnuts.

4 Scrape the mixture into the prepared tin, sprinkle over the remaining hazelnuts and the demerara sugar and then bake in the preheated oven for about 25–30 minutes until golden and firm yet springy to the touch.

5 Leave to cool a little in the tin before turning out and slicing. Delicious served warm.

PASSION FRUIT BUTTER CAKE

Delicious and incredibly moreish, this is the kind of cake to which you have to keep sneaking back and slicing off just one more tiny piece… to check it really is as nice as you thought it was!

SERVES 6–8

MAKING TIME
15 minutes

BAKING TIME
45 minutes

250 g unsalted butter, softened

225 g caster sugar

3 large eggs

240 g self-raising flour

100 ml semi-skimmed milk

pulp of 4 passion fruit (strain to remove the seeds)

For the icing

225 g icing sugar

pulp and seeds from 2 passion fruit

1 Preheat the oven to 180°C (350°F/Gas 4) and line a 20-cm round cake tin with a cake tin liner or use non-stick baking paper.

2 Cream together the butter and sugar then beat in the eggs; whisk at high speed to incorporate lots of air.

3 Fold in the flour, then the milk and passion fruit pulp. Scrape into the prepared tin and smooth to level. Bake in the preheated oven for 45 minutes until golden and firm to the touch and a skewer inserted into the centre comes out clean.

4 To make the icing, put the icing sugar in a bowl and scrape in the seeds and pulp from the passion fruit. Use a knife to stir into the icing sugar, it will seem too dry at first but keep mixing and don't be tempted to add anything until you are absolutely sure it needs more liquid. If the icing is too stiff, add a tiny bit more of the seeds left over from the cake.

5 Take the cake out of the oven and allow to cool before removing from the tin and spreading with the icing.

SCRUMPTIOUS CHOCOLATE FUDGE CAKE

Dense, moist and scrumptious chocolate fudge cake, this is adapted from a recipe by my friend Rosie and I bake it all the time. Paul Hollywood said he loved this when I made it on *The Great British Bake Off*.

SERVES 8	MAKING TIME	BAKING TIME
	20 minutes	35–40 minutes

215 g plain chocolate, chopped
215 g chilled unsalted butter, diced
125 ml water
100 g self-raising flour
70 g plain flour, sifted
30 g cocoa powder
215 g light muscovado sugar
215 g caster sugar
3 large eggs
75 ml crème fraîche

For the chocolate ganache
300 g plain chocolate (I use Bournville)
300 ml double cream

1 Preheat the oven to 170°C (325°F/Gas 3) and line a 23-cm round sandwich cake tin with a cake tin liner. You need one that covers the base and goes up the sides of the tin as this batter is very liquid.

2 Melt the chocolate, butter and water together in a bowl set over a pan of simmering water; leave to cool slightly.

3 Sift the flours and cocoa powder into a bowl and then stir in both sugars. Beat the eggs with the crème fraîche and then add to the dry ingredients along with the melted chocolate mixture. Mix everything together until smooth.

4 Pour into the prepared tin and bake in the preheated oven for 35–40 minutes. The cake will not rise much but should feel fairly firm to the touch. Leave to cool completely in the tin.

5 Make the ganache. Put the chocolate and cream into a bowl set over a pan of simmering water to melt. Stir together and allow to cool to a spreading consistency. Spread the top of the cooled cake with chocolate ganache.

Double the recipe to make two 23-cm cakes. Decorate the top of each cake with ganache and cover with crumbled flake bars. Enjoy one cake and wrap the other tightly in cling film and foil and freeze for another day. Defrost for about 4 hours at room temperature. Pop in the microwave for 2 mins to make it extra fudgy.

Double the recipe above to make a layered chocolate fudge cake. Sandwich the two cakes together with about one-third of the ganache and spread the remainder over the top and sides in a thick layer. Makes a great party cake decorated with truffles, fresh or sugar flowers or piles of summer fruit.

Use the recipe above to make delicious chocolate fudge cupcakes (makes 12). Bake for about 20 minutes then spread with ganache when cool.

FLOURLESS RICH CHOCOLATE ALMOND CAKE

This delicious cake has been in the family recipe book since the 1940s. My husband's grandmother, Prue, a vicar's wife and fabulous cake baker, used to make this cake for vicarage teas and family birthday parties. I think she would be thrilled to know it is still one of our favourite cakes.

SERVES 6–8	MAKING TIME	BAKING TIME
	20 minutes	20 minutes

170 g plain chocolate (check the label to make sure it's gluten free)

5 large eggs, separated

170 g unsalted butter, softened

85 g caster sugar

140 g ground almonds

1 tsp gluten-free baking powder

For the icing

200 g icing sugar

1 tbsp gluten-free cocoa powder

2 tsp instant coffee powder

1 tbsp boiling water

85 g unsalted butter

1 Preheat the oven to 180°C (350°F/Gas 4). Line two 18-cm round cake tins with cake tin liners or non-stick baking paper.

2 Put the chocolate in a heatproof bowl and pop in the oven to melt as it preheats – this will take about 5 minutes.

3 Put the egg whites into the bowl of an electric mixer and whisk to stiff peaks. While they are whisking, put the butter and sugar in a large bowl and use a balloon whisk to cream them together. Then add the egg yolks, ground almonds, baking powder and melted chocolate and mix well to combine.

4 Fold the stiff egg whites into the chocolate mixture then scrape into the prepared tins. Bake in the preheated oven for about 20 minutes until firm to the touch. Remove from the oven and leave to cool in their tins for about 10 minutes before transferring to a wire rack.

5 Make the icing. Sift the icing sugar into the bowl of a food processor or a large bowl. Mix the cocoa and coffee powder into a paste with the boiling water and add to the icing sugar with the butter. Beat well or whizz until smooth. Add a little more boiling water if the icing is too stiff.

6 Once the cakes are cool, spread half the icing on to one of the cakes and sandwich together. Top the cake with the remaining icing.

VANILLA CAKE WITH
MILKY CHOCOLATE GANACHE

A buttery, vanilla-infused sponge – made with only the yolk of the egg – sandwiched with the milkiest chocolate ganache. If you are looking for even greater indulgence, double the quantity of ganache and slather it on top as well. This is a great cake to bake if you have made meringues and want to use up the spare egg yolks.

SERVES 6–8

MAKING TIME
20 minutes

BAKING TIME
30 minutes

170 g unsalted butter, softened
265 g caster sugar
6 large egg yolks
300 g self-raising flour
3 tsp baking powder
240 ml semi-skimmed milk
2 tsp vanilla extract
seeds from 1 vanilla pod (optional)
icing sugar, for dusting

For the icing
200 g good-quality milk chocolate
  (I use Green & Blacks' milk
  chocolate for cooking)
100 ml double cream

1 Preheat the oven to 180°C (350°F/Gas 4). Lightly oil two 18-cm round loose-bottomed cake tins and then dust with flour. Alternatively line with non-stick baking paper.

2 Make the icing. Break the chocolate into a heatproof bowl and place over a pan of simmering water; the bottom of the bowl should not touch the water. As soon as the chocolate starts to melt add the cream and stir together. Beat well with a wooden spoon and remove from the heat to stand and firm up a little.

3 Cream together the butter and sugar in an electric mixer, using the whisk attachment. Add the egg yolks and whisk well.

4 Mix in all the remaining ingredients, except the icing sugar, until everything is combined, stopping to scrape down the sides of the bowl. Spoon the mixture into the prepared tins and bake in the preheated oven for about 30 minutes. Check whether the cake is done by inserting a skewer or sharp knife into the centre; it should come out clean.

5 Remove the cakes from the oven and leave to cool in their tins for at least 10 minutes. Then, remove from the tins and place on a cooling rack to cool completely before sandwiching together with the chocolate icing and dusting with icing sugar.

THOMAS' CARROTY CAKE

When Thomas was just three years old, he told me this was his favourite cake. He loves to make it with me, and always ensures there is a thick layer of cream cheese icing in the middle and on top.

SERVES 6–8

MAKING TIME
15–20 minutes (longer if making with children)

BAKING TIME
20–25 minutes

250 g light soft brown sugar

250 ml sunflower or vegetable oil

3 large eggs, lightly beaten

2 tsp vanilla extract

250 g self-raising flour

1 tsp baking powder

½ tsp salt

1 tsp mixed spice

1 tsp vanilla extract

1–2 tsp grated orange zest

300 g carrots, peeled and coarsely grated

100 g sultanas

75 g walnut pieces (optional – Thomas would not allow these in his cake)

For the cream cheese icing

150 g full-fat cream cheese

40 g unsalted butter, softened

1 tbsp orange juice

1 tsp vanilla extract

500 g icing sugar

1 Preheat the oven to 170°C (325°F/Gas 3). Line two 20-cm loose-bottomed cake tins with cake tin liners or use non-stick baking paper.

2 Put all the ingredients for the cake in the bowl of an electric mixer and mix until well combined, although Thomas mixes this in a large bowl with a wooden spoon.

3 Scrape the mixture into the prepared tins and bake in the preheated oven for 20–25 minutes until golden and firm yet springy to the touch.

4 Prepare the cream cheese icing. Put the cream cheese, butter, orange juice and vanilla into a bowl with half the icing sugar and beat well with an electric hand-held whisk; alternatively whizz in a food processor. Add the remaining icing sugar and whisk or whizz until smooth and fluffy – this will take about 3 minutes.

5 Remove the cakes from the oven and allow to cool before sandwiching together with the icing.

GOOSEBERRY AND ELDERFLOWER SPONGE

The lightest butter-free sponge cake you can imagine, softly scented with elderflower, and filled with poached gooseberries and elderflower whipped cream. You can taste the English summertime in every mouthful.

SERVES 6–8	MAKING TIME	BAKING TIME
	20–25 minutes	10 minutes

100 g caster sugar

4 large eggs

100 g self-raising flour, sifted

1 tsp baking powder

1 tsp grated lemon zest

2 tbsp elderflower cordial

For the filling

100 ml whipping cream

1 tbsp elderflower cordial

200 g gooseberries

40 g caster sugar

1 tbsp water

Miranda's variations

This butter-free sponge cake can be adapted to include other flavours and ingredients:

For a delicious raspberry version, substitute raspberries for the gooseberries.

For a simpler and healthier Victoria sponge, sandwich together with jam and sprinkle the top with a little caster sugar.

For a chocolate version, make a filling using margarine, icing sugar, cocoa powder and a little boiling water, and make a glaze for the top from cocoa powder, icing sugar and a little boiling water.

1 Preheat the oven to 180°C (350°F/Gas 4). Line two 20-cm sandwich cake tins with cake tin liners or non-stick baking paper.

2 Put the sugar and eggs in the bowl of an electric mixer and whisk on a high speed for 3–4 minutes; the mixture should triple in size.

3 Gently fold in the flour and baking powder then fold in the lemon zest.

4 Scrape into the prepared tins and bake in the preheated oven for about 10 minutes until pale golden, springy and coming away from the sides of the tin. As soon as the cakes come out of the oven, sprinkle with the elderflower cordial and leave to cool in their tins for about 5 minutes before transferring to a cooling rack.

5 Prepare the filling. Whip the cream until thick then fold in the elderflower cordial; set aside.

6 Put the gooseberries, sugar and water into a small pan and cook until the gooseberries have softened but still hold their shape. Use a slotted spoon to lift the gooseberries into a bowl. Increase the heat and boil the juicy syrup for a few minutes until it thickens. Leave to cool.

7 To serve, put one cake on a serving plate, spread with a thick layer of gooseberries, then a generous layer of elderflower cream. Put the other cake on top and pour the cooled gooseberry syrup over the top to glaze. Alternatively, simply dust with icing sugar and sprinkle with elderflower blossom or a few fresh flowers.

MALTESERS® CAKE

The perfect cake to make with children, or to enjoy when you need a comforting and homely treat! My family loves this gently malted and subtly chocolatey cake, and I hope you will enjoy it too.

SERVES 6–8

MAKING TIME
20 minutes

BAKING TIME
20 minutes

60 g milk chocolate

200 g unsalted butter, softened

200 g caster sugar

4 large eggs, lightly beaten

150 g self-raising flour

40 g malted drink powder (I use Horlicks)

25 g cocoa powder, sifted

1 tsp baking powder

Maltesers, to decorate

For the icing

300 g icing sugar

125 g unsalted butter, softened

50 g malted drink powder (I use Horlicks)

50 g cocoa powder, sifted

4–6 tbsp semi-skimmed milk

1 Preheat the oven to 180°C (350°F/Gas 4). Line two 20-cm round loose-bottomed cake tins with cake tin liners or non-stick baking paper.

2 Put the chocolate in a heatproof bowl and pop in the oven to melt as it preheats – this will take about 5 minutes.

3 Cream the butter and sugar together then add the eggs a little at a time, beating well after each addition.

4 Gently fold in the flour, malted drink powder, cocoa and baking powder until completely incorporated. Then fold in the melted chocolate.

5 Scrape into the prepared tins and bake in the preheated oven for about 20 minutes, until springy to the touch, dry on top and coming away from the sides of the tin; a skewer inserted into the centre should come out clean. Leave to cool in their tins or turn out on to a wire rack to cool completely.

6 Make the icing. Place all the ingredients into a food processor and blend until smooth and creamy. Add a little more milk if the mixture is too stiff. Sandwich and top the cakes with a generous amount of icing and decorate the top with Maltesers.

WHITE CHOCOLATE AND LEMON CAKE

This cake looks very impressive, but is a whizz to make. It is baked in a tray bake tin, and then sliced in half lengthways – I find this far speedier than baking two individual cakes.

SERVES 8	MAKING TIME	BAKING TIME
	30 minutes	15–20 minutes

4 large eggs

200 g caster sugar

grated zest and juice of
  2 lemons

200 g plain flour

1 tsp baking powder

icing sugar, for dusting

raspberries, to decorate
  (optional)

For the filling

400 g white chocolate,
  broken into small pieces

pinch of salt

100 ml double cream

200 ml whipping cream

8–10 tbsp lemon curd, plus
  1 tbsp extra to decorate

1 Preheat the oven to 180°C (350°F/Gas 4). Line a 20 x 30-cm tray bake tin with a cake tin liner or non-stick baking paper.

2 Whisk the eggs in the bowl of an electric mixer until pale yellow and fluffy, this will take about 4 minutes. Add the sugar and whisk again until pale and thick; this will take a further 4 minutes.

3 Use a large spoon to fold in the lemon zest (reserving a little to decorate), flour and baking powder, then fold in 2 tablespoons of the lemon juice.

4 Spoon into the tin and spread to level out. Bake in the preheated oven for 15–20 minutes until golden and firm yet springy to the touch.

5 When the cake comes out of the oven, spoon the remaining lemon juice over the top and leave to cool in the tin for at least 15 minutes.

6 Make the filling. Put the white chocolate, salt and double cream in a bowl over a pan of simmering water. As soon as the chocolate starts to melt, stir and keep stirring until the chocolate has melted and you have a creamy mixture.

7 Remove from the heat and beat with a wooden spoon. Leave to cool and firm up at room temperature – it will be quite runny at this stage but after about half an hour will become firmer.

8 When the cake is cold slice in half lengthways to make two rectangles. Whip the whipping cream to soft peaks. Spread lemon curd over one of the cakes, then top with the white chocolate ganache and then the whipped cream. Put the other cake on top. Drizzle with the remaining lemon curd, grated lemon zest and dust with icing sugar. Decorate with a few raspberries, if using.

COFFEE AND WALNUT CAKE

Comforting coffee sponge, creamy buttercream and crumbly walnuts packed into every thick slice.

SERVES 8–10	MAKING TIME	BAKING TIME
	25 minutes	25 minutes

225 g unsalted butter, softened

225 g caster sugar

4 large eggs, lightly beaten

225 g self-raising flour

2 tsp baking powder

100 g walnuts

2 tbsp instant coffee mixed
with 2 tbsp boiling water

For the buttercream

200 g unsalted butter, softened

550 g icing sugar

3 tsp instant coffee mixed
with a little hot water

2–3 tbsp semi-skimmed milk

For the topping

150 g whole walnuts

grated chocolate or
chocolate sprinkles

1 Preheat the oven to 180°C (350°F/Gas 4) and line a 20 x 30-cm tray bake tin with non-stick baking paper.

2 Cream together the butter and sugar in an electric mixer until pale and golden. Add the beaten eggs to the mixture a little at a time, whisking well after each addition.

3 Sift in the flour and baking powder and then gently fold into the mix with a large metal spoon.

4 Gently crush half of the walnuts and leave the rest in small pieces. Fold all the walnuts into the cake mixture along with the coffee and water mixture.

5 Spoon into the prepared tin and bake in the preheated oven for about 25 minutes until firm yet springy to the touch.

6 While the cake is in the oven make the buttercream. Put the butter, half the icing sugar, the coffee mixture and the milk into a food processor or mixer and mix until creamy – this will take about 2 minutes on a high speed. Add the remaining icing sugar and then mix again.

7 Remove the cake from the oven and leave to cool in the tin for at least 10 minutes before transferring to a wire rack. Once the cake is completely cold, use a sharp knife to slice the cake in half lengthways to make two long thin rectangles (you may want to trim the edges to make them tidy and straight).

8 Place one cake rectangle on a clean piece of baking paper, spread with half the buttercream and place the other rectangle on top. Use a palette knife to cover the top of the cake with the remaining buttercream. Decorate with the whole walnuts and grated chocolate or chocolate sprinkles.

GLORIOUSLY STICKY TOFFEE CAKE

Sticky toffee pudding in a cake (see page 2) – need I say more?

SERVES 10	MAKING TIME	BAKING TIME
	20–25 minutes	30 minutes

375 g dates

250 ml water

2 tsp bicarbonate of soda

4 large eggs

250 g muscovado sugar

2 tbsp golden syrup

200 g unsalted butter, melted

2 tsp vanilla extract

350 g self-raising flour

pinch of salt

For the icing

200 g unsalted butter

400 g icing sugar

4 tbsp dulce de leche
(I use Nestlé Carnation Caramel)

2 tbsp semi-skimmed milk (you may
not need this much)

For the topping

4 tbsp dulce de leche
(I use Nestlé Carnation Caramel)

handful of fudge pieces,
roughly chopped

1 Preheat the oven to 180°C (350°F/Gas 4). Line two 18-cm round cake tins with non-stick baking paper or lightly oil and dust with flour.

2 Put the dates in a pan, cover with the water and bring to the boil. Add the bicarbonate of soda, remove from the heat and stir well. Transfer the contents of the pan to a food processor and whizz until smooth; alternatively use a hand-held electric blender or mash by hand.

3 Use an electric hand-held whisk to whisk together the eggs, sugar and syrup until pale and fluffy. Whisk in the melted butter and then gently mix in the vanilla and puréed dates.

4 Use a metal spoon to fold in the flour and salt. Spoon half of the mixture into each tin, level and place in the preheated oven for about 30 minutes. Check whether the cake is done by inserting a skewer or sharp knife into the centre; it should come out clean. Leave to cool in their tins.

5 Make the icing. Beat together the butter, icing sugar and caramel. Add the milk a little at a time until you have a creamy consistency.

6 Generously sandwich the cakes together with the icing and spread a thick layer on top. Drizzle with the caramel for the topping and sprinkle with fudge chunks before serving.

To serve as a pudding, warm the caramel for the topping gently to create a hot toffee sauce – serve with scoops of good-quality vanilla ice cream. You could also bake this in a tray-bake tin and serve warm, cut into squares. Make double the toffee sauce and drizzle over the top to serve.

BLUEBERRY AND LEMON YOGHURT CAKE

A delicious squidgy cake, studded with blueberries and drizzled with lemon icing. The yoghurt gives a freshness to the cake, and the lemon a zestiness. This is also excellent made with raspberries.

SERVES 6–8

MAKING TIME
15 minutes

BAKING TIME
1 hour

225 g caster sugar

3 large eggs

225 g Greek yoghurt

225 g self-raising flour

1 tsp baking powder

grated zest of 1 lemon

50 g unsalted butter, melted

150 g blueberries

For the icing

200 g icing sugar

2–3 tsp lemon juice

1 Preheat the oven to 180°C (350°F/Gas 4). Line a deep 20-cm springform cake tin with a cake tin liner or use non-stick baking paper.

2 Whisk together the sugar and eggs in an electric mixer on a high speed for about 4 minutes until thick and voluminous.

3 Fold in the yoghurt then add the flour, baking powder, lemon zest, half the blueberries and melted butter and fold again. Scrape into the prepared tin and sprinkle the remaining blueberries over the top.

4 Bake on a low shelf in the preheated oven for about 45 minutes or until the cake is golden on top and a skewer comes out clean.

5 To make the icing use a knife to mix together the icing sugar and lemon juice, adding the lemon juice a little at a time. Remove the cake from the oven and allow to cool in the tin for about 20 minutes. Use a palette knife or spoon to spread the icing all over the cake.

LITTLE
CAKES

'EARLY BIRD' MUFFINS

I am often up doing the early shift; with three small children, lie-ins are a thing of the past! I love to turn my frustration at being hauled from happy slumber into baking heaven, and the fact that this recipe provides breakfast too is doubly good. I make these muffins with whatever happens to be in the fruit bowl.

MAKES 12	MAKING TIME	BAKING TIME
	10 minutes (longer if making with children!)	15–20 minutes

145 g soft brown sugar

80 g oats

170 g self-raising flour

1 tsp bicarbonate of soda

45 g dried apricots and/or sultanas, chopped

1 peach or nectarine, roughly chopped (you could also use strawberries)

½ banana, mashed with a fork

2 large eggs

200 ml semi-skimmed milk

80 g unsalted butter, melted

For the topping

20 g oats

2 tbsp demerara sugar

1 Preheat the oven to 170°C (325°F/Gas 3) and line a 12-hole muffin tray with paper cases or squares of baking paper.

2 Put all the dry ingredients into a bowl and stir with a wooden spoon to combine. Add the dried and fresh fruit and stir through.

3 Lightly beat the eggs in a jug and then add the milk and melted butter.

4 Make a well in the middle of the mixing bowl and pour in the milk, egg and butter mixture. Stir well with a wooden spoon until just combined – don't over mix.

5 Spoon into the prepared muffin cases. Mix together the oats and sugar for the topping and then sprinkle a little over the top of each muffin. Bake in the preheated oven for 20–25 minutes, until golden and springy to the touch.

SYRUP BUNS

These surely are the taste of childhood – there is nothing like the rich, mellow, nostalgic taste of golden syrup. These are little buns full of comfort.

MAKES ABOUT 12	MAKING TIME	BAKING TIME
	10 minutes	15–20 minutes

250 g unsalted butter

250 g caster sugar

3 large eggs, lightly beaten

300 ml golden syrup, plus
a few tbsp for drizzling

500 g self-raising flour

100 ml semi-skimmed milk

1 Preheat the oven to 180°C (350°F/Gas 4) and line a 12-hole muffin tray with paper cases.

2 Cream together the butter and sugar and then beat in the eggs.

3 Warm the syrup in a microwave for about 20 seconds (or in a small pan over a low heat) and then add to the mixture and beat well. Gently mix in the flour then add the milk and mix to combine.

4 Spoon into the prepared cases and bake in the preheated oven for 15–20 minutes or until golden and springy to the touch.

5 Remove from the oven and immediately spoon a teaspoonful of syrup on to each bun. Leave to cool a little in their trays before enjoying as soon as possible.

This is also delicious as a pudding – serve warm with a dollop of vanilla ice cream on top or with lashings of custard.

HONEY, CINNAMON AND RAISIN BUNS

Gobble these straight from the oven with a glass of cold milk! Great for after-school snacks and for walks in the woods.

MAKES 12	MAKING TIME	BAKING TIME
	15 minutes	15–20 minutes

150 g unsalted butter

3 large eggs

110 g soft light brown sugar

150 g self-raising flour

pinch of salt

1½ tsp baking powder

1 tsp ground cinnamon

4 tbsp clear honey

100 g raisins

1 Preheat the oven to 180°C (350°F/Gas 4) and line a 12-hole muffin tray with paper cases.

2 Melt the butter; about 30 seconds in the microwave will be enough, or in a small pan over a low heat.

3 Put the eggs and sugar into the bowl of an electric mixer and whisk on a high speed for about 3 minutes, or until pale and thick.

4 Gently mix in the flour, salt, baking powder and cinnamon. Use a spoon to fold in the melted butter, honey and raisins.

5 Spoon into the prepared cases and bake in the preheated oven for 15–20 minutes until golden and springy to the touch. Delicious eaten warm.

MILK AND BLACKBERRY BUNNIES

Perfect for tired and mischievous 'flopsy bunnies' at the end of a busy day.

MAKES 12	MAKING TIME	BAKING TIME
	10 minutes	15 minutes

180 g unsalted butter
180 g caster sugar
3 large eggs, lightly beaten
180 g self-raising flour
pinch of salt
1 tsp baking powder
100 ml semi-skimmed milk
100 g blackberries
  or blueberries

1 Preheat the oven to 180°C (350°F/Gas 4) and line a 12-hole muffin tray with paper cases.

2 Cream together the butter and sugar and beat in the eggs.

3 Mix in the flour, salt and baking powder, then add the milk and beat well to make a smooth batter. Mix in the blackberries or blueberries.

4 Pour or spoon into the paper cases and bake in the preheated oven for 15 minutes until golden and springy to the touch.

NOTE

More often than not we make these with blueberries instead of blackberries as we usually always have some in the fridge.

ORANGE CHOCOLATE CHIP ROCK CAKES

Perfect for snacks, picnics and lunch boxes, or for munching on while rushing around in the garden recreating childhood storybook adventures! These are best eaten warm.

MAKES 16	MAKING TIME	BAKING TIME
	10 minutes	15–20 minutes

225 g self-raising flour
pinch of salt
85 g chilled unsalted butter, finely diced
grated zest of 1 orange
1 large egg
85 g caster sugar
2 tbsp semi-skimmed milk
100 g chocolate chips

1 Preheat the oven to 180°C (350°F/Gas 4) and line two shallow baking sheets with non-stick baking paper.

2 Sift the flour and salt into a large mixing bowl and rub in the butter with your fingertips. Alternatively, whizz in a food processor.

3 Add the orange zest, egg, sugar and milk and mix well to combine (using a knife if mixing by hand). Stir in the chocolate chips and roll into balls (about the size of an egg). Put the balls on to the prepared baking sheets, making sure they are well spaced.

4 Bake in the preheated oven for 15–20 minutes; the bottom of the cakes should come away cleanly and be golden in colour.

ICED BUNS

Perfect for walks, picnics and after-school treats. One of my fondest childhood memories is of licking the icing off the paper bags the buns came in. This is a cheat's way to make them without having to wait for bread dough to rest and prove.

MAKES 12	MAKING TIME	BAKING TIME
	15 minutes	20 minutes

285 ml semi-skimmed milk

2 large eggs

340 g self-raising flour

½ tsp salt

55 g unsalted butter

85 g caster sugar

150 g sultanas or raisins

12 glacé cherries

For the icing

200 g icing sugar

1–2 tsp water

1 Preheat the oven to 190°C (375°/Gas 5) and line a 12-hole muffin tray with paper cases or squares of non-stick baking paper.

2 Put the milk and eggs into a jug and beat together with a fork to combine.

3 Put the flour and salt into a bowl and rub in the butter with your fingers; alternatively whizz in a food processor. Stir in the sugar and sultanas or raisins.

4 Mix in the beaten egg and milk, then spoon the mixture into the prepared cases.

5 Bake in the preheated oven for 15–20 minutes until golden and springy to the touch. Take out of the oven and leave in the muffin tray to cool.

6 Put the icing sugar in a bowl and add the water, a little at a time, until you have a thick, glossy icing. Spoon a dollop of the icing on to each cooled bun. Press a cherry on top of each bun.

CHOCOLATE PUDDLE CAKES

My children love to make and devour these little chocolate cakes. Hide a piece of chocolate in each before baking to create a chocolate puddle inside. As soon as the cakes come out of the oven, pop a chocolate button on top, to make a puddle on top too. Best eaten warm.

MAKES 12	MAKING TIME	BAKING TIME
	10 minutes	15–20 minutes

150 g unsalted butter, softened

150 g caster sugar

3 large eggs, lightly beaten

225 g self-raising flour

1½ tsp baking powder

30 g cocoa powder

1½ tbsp semi-skimmed milk

24 chunks of milk chocolate

12 giant chocolate buttons

1 Preheat the oven to 180°C (350°F/Gas 4) and line a 12-hole muffin tray with paper cases.

2 Put all the ingredients except the chocolate chunks and buttons into a mixing bowl and beat with a wooden spoon until well combined.

3 Put a dessertspoon of mixture into each case and top with two chunks of chocolate. Cover with the remaining mixture then use a knife to smooth and flatten the tops.

4 Bake in the preheated oven for about 15–20 minutes. Remove from the oven and while still in the tin, place one chocolate button on top of each hot cake.

For a more grown-up version, use 200 g of self-raising flour and 55 g of cocoa powder in the cake mixture, and replace the chocolate buttons and milk chocolate chunks with 70% cocoa solids chocolate or a piece of your favourite chocolate bar.

ICED LEMON AND POPPY SEED CAKES

There is something addictive about the union of sharp lemon and crunchy poppy seeds. The ground almonds, used here instead of flour, make these little cakes extra moist as well as gluten-free, and the lemon icing creates a pretty glaze on top.

MAKES AT LEAST 12	MAKING TIME	BAKING TIME
	10 minutes	20–25 minutes

180 g unsalted butter, softened

180 g caster sugar

grated zest of 1 lemon

4 large eggs, lightly beaten

250 g ground almonds

2 tbsp poppy seeds

2 tsp gluten-free baking powder

For the icing

grated zest and juice of 1 lemon

150 g icing sugar

1 Preheat the oven to 170°C (325°/Gas 3) and line a 12-hole muffin tray with paper cases.

2 Cream together the butter, sugar and lemon zest.

3 Beat in the eggs and then fold in the almonds, poppy seeds and baking powder.

4 Spoon into the prepared cases, smooth the tops with a palette knife and then bake in the preheated oven for 20–25 minutes, until golden and springy to the touch.

5 Mix the icing ingredients together in a bowl and spoon over the cakes once they are completely cold.

NOTE

To make crystallised lemon zest, use a zester to remove thin strips of rind from the lemon, toss in caster sugar and leave to firm up a little before sprinkling over the top of the cakes.

CORNISH SAFFRON BUNS

Made with saffron-infused milk and packed with currants, these little buns are a lovely alternative to scones. Traditionally from Cornwall, saffron buns usually require the patience of breadmaking, but this version can be made in a jiffy. Delicious with jam and clotted cream, or straight from the oven, thickly spread with butter.

MAKES 12	MAKING TIME	BAKING TIME
	10 minutes	20 minutes

285 ml semi-skimmed milk
½ tsp saffron strands
340 g self-raising flour
½ tsp salt
55 g unsalted butter
85 g caster sugar
200 g currants
2 large eggs, lightly beaten

1 Preheat the oven to 190°C (375°/Gas 5) and line a 12-hole muffin tray with paper cases or squares of baking paper.

2 Put the milk and saffron into a pan and warm gently. Remove from the heat and leave to infuse while you get on with the rest of the recipe.

3 Put the flour and salt into a bowl and rub in the butter with your fingers; alternatively whizz in a food processor. Stir in the sugar and currants.

4 Pour the saffron milk through a sieve to strain and add to the mixture with the beaten eggs. Mix until combined and then spoon the mixture into the prepared cases.

5 Bake in the preheated oven for 20 minutes. These are best enjoyed straight from the oven.

SIMPLE LITTLE GINGERBREAD CAKES

Sugar and spice and all things nice… that's what these little cakes are made of!

MAKES 12	MAKING TIME	BAKING TIME
	15 minutes	15–20 minutes

175 g unsalted butter, softened
175 g dark brown sugar
3 large eggs
1½ tsp baking powder
2 tsp ground ginger
1 tsp mixed spice
75 ml semi-skimmed milk

For the icing (optional)
325 g icing sugar
1 tbsp golden syrup
20 g unsalted butter
2 tbsp hot water

1 Preheat the oven to 180°C (350°F/Gas 4) and line a 12-hole muffin tray with paper cases.

2 Put all the cake ingredients into a large bowl or the bowl of an electric mixer, and mix well to combine.

3 Spoon into the prepared cases and bake in the preheated oven for 15–20 minutes, until dark golden and springy to the touch.

4 Make the icing, if using. Put the icing sugar in a heatproof bowl and stir in the golden syrup, butter and water. Put the bowl over a pan of simmering water and stir to make a smooth icing. When the cakes are cool, cover with the icing.

These are also delicious as a pudding, un-iced and served with custard.

CHOCOLATE CUPCAKES WITH STICKY CHOCOLATE GANACHE

Sweet figs and apricots, along with dried fruit and citrusy zest, are the perfect companions in these gluten-free chocolate cakes. The sticky chocolate ganache is the crowning glory, and ensures these cupcakes are loved by all those who eat them. A fantastic recipe to enjoy throughout the year, but a particularly lovely alternative to Christmas cake or pudding.

MAKES 24	MAKING TIME	BAKING TIME
	15 minutes	20–25 minutes

100 g dried figs, chopped

100 g dried apricots, chopped

grated zest and juice of 1 lemon

grated zest and juice of 1 orange

6 large eggs

200 g caster sugar

200 g ground almonds

25 g gluten-free cocoa powder

1 tsp gluten-free baking powder

50 g dried cranberries

100 g dried fruit (sultanas, currants, raisins)

100 g chocolate chips (milk or plain, check the label to make sure it's gluten free)

For the sticky chocolate topping

200 g plain chocolate (check the label to make sure it's gluten free)

100 ml double cream

2 tbsp dulce de leche (I use Nestlé Carnation Caramel)

1 Preheat the oven to 180°C (350°F/Gas 4) and line two 12-hole muffin trays with paper cases.

2 Put the figs, apricots and lemon and orange zest into a small saucepan. Put the lemon and orange juice in a measuring jug and add enough water to make the liquid up to 200 ml. Add this to the pan and simmer over a low heat until almost all the water has been absorbed by the fruit.

3 Whisk the eggs in an electric mixer fitted with a balloon whisk attachment for about 3 minutes, until they are pale and fluffy. Add the sugar, a little at a time, whisking after each addition until it has all been incorporated.

4 Use a metal spoon to fold in the dry ingredients then gently fold in the poached figs and apricots, dried fruit and chocolate chips.

5 Spoon the mixture into the prepared cases, no more than two-thirds full. Level the tops and bake in the preheated oven for 20–25 minutes, or until springy to the touch. Leave to cool in the trays.

6 Make the topping. Put the chocolate and cream in a bowl over a pan of simmering water. Once the chocolate has melted, stir together then add the caramel and stir again. Leave to cool and thicken a little before spreading on top of the cakes.

If you are making these for Christmas, add 1 teaspoon of mixed spice to the flour.

CHOCOLATE JAMMY FLAKE BARS

These jammy flake bars were my favourite choice from our much-loved bakers when we were little. My heart skipped a beat when, on holiday in Devon, we discovered a shop where the baker was hand-dipping the cakes in chocolate. This is my quick and easy version.

MAKES ABOUT 18	MAKING TIME	BAKING TIME
	20 minutes	20–25 minutes

225 g unsalted butter

225 g caster sugar

4 large eggs

2 tsp vanilla extract

150 g self-raising flour

2 tsp baking powder

80 g cocoa powder, sifted

50 ml semi-skimmed milk

8 tbsp strawberry jam

200 g plain chocolate, such as Bournville

6 Flake bars, each broken into three

These are pretty served as a tea party treat in little paper cake cases.

1 Preheat the oven to 180°C (350°F/Gas 4) and line a 20 x 30-cm tray bake tin with non-stick baking paper.

2 Put the butter, sugar, eggs and vanilla in the bowl of an electric mixer and cream together. Add the flour, baking powder and cocoa powder and beat well to combine. Add the milk, and mix again.

3 Spoon half the mixture into the prepared tin and spread to make a thin layer. Dollop the jam across the mixture then spread with a palette knife. Add the remaining cake mixture and spread to level and cover the jam.

4 Bake in the preheated oven for 20–25 minutes or until springy to the touch and coming away from the edges of the tin. Leave to cool in the tin for about 30 minutes. Then lift the cake out of the tin, still in its baking paper, and stand on a chopping board.

5 While the cake is in the oven, melt the chocolate in the microwave or in a bowl over a pan of simmering water. Remove from the heat and leave to cool a little.

6 Use a sharp knife to cut the cake into about 18 portions. Spoon the melted chocolate over each cake in a thick layer. Press the Flake pieces into the chocolate on each cake while the chocolate is still soft. Leave to set or, if impatient, eat messily while still warm!

LITTLE BAKEWELL CAKES

These little almond cakes are baked with a hidden pool of raspberry jam inside and then decorated with pure white almond icing, slithers of flaked almonds and a glacé cherry.

MAKES 16	MAKING TIME	BAKING TIME
	15 minutes	15–20 minutes

250 g unsalted butter, softened
250 g caster sugar
4 large eggs
150 g self-raising flour
100 g ground almonds
1 tsp almond extract
5 tbsp semi-skimmed milk
about 150 g raspberry jam

For the topping
100 g icing sugar
1 tsp almond extract
1–2 tsp water
16 glacé cherries
50 g flaked almonds, toasted

1 Preheat the oven to 180°C (350°F/Gas 4) and line a 16-hole muffin tray (or two trays) with paper cases.

2 Whisk together the butter and sugar in an electric mixer, then add the eggs and whisk on high speed to combine (or, if making by hand, use a balloon whisk).

3 Gently mix in all the flour, ground almonds, almond extract and milk.

4 Half-fill the prepared cases with the mixture and then drop a spoon of raspberry jam on top (roughly 1 teaspoon of jam per cake). Cover the jam with the remaining mixture and smooth the tops over with a palette knife.

5 Bake in the preheated oven for 15–20 minutes or until pale golden and springy to the touch. Leave in the tins to cool before transferring to a wire rack to cool completely.

6 Mix together the icing sugar and almond extract with a little water to make a thick, smooth icing. Spoon the icing on to each cake, pop a cherry on top and sprinkle with toasted almonds.

CRANBERRY CUPCAKES WITH WHITE CHOCOLATE BUTTERCREAM

This is a simple but delicious alternative to Christmas cake. The cupcakes look pretty and very festive so are fantastic for parties – but good enough to enjoy as a teatime treat at any time of year!

MAKES ABOUT 24	MAKING TIME	BAKING TIME
	25 minutes	12 minutes

250 g unsalted butter, softened

250 g caster sugar

grated zest of 1 orange

4 large eggs, lightly beaten

250 g self-raising flour

5 tbsp semi-skimmed milk

100 g dried cranberries

24 fresh cranberries, to decorate, or sugar-paste holly decorations

For the orange soak (optional)

2 tbsp icing sugar

juice of 1 orange

For the white chocolate buttercream

450 g icing sugar, sifted

100 g unsalted butter, softened

50 ml semi-skimmed milk

1 tsp vanilla extract

100 g white chocolate, melted in a bowl over a pan of simmering water

TIP

These freeze really well so make a batch in advance and pop them (un-iced) into the freezer, ready for unexpected guests at Christmas. Wait until they have fully defrosted before decorating.

1 Preheat the oven to 180°C (350°F/Gas 4) and line two 12-hole muffin trays with paper cases.

2 Cream together the butter, sugar and orange zest – for really light cupcakes always use a balloon whisk or the whisk attachment on your electric mixer. Add the eggs, roughly one egg at a time, whisking after each addition.

3 Once the eggs are well combined, gradually sift in the flour and gently fold in with a large metal spoon (taking extra care to fold gently to keep all the air in the mixture).

4 Fold in the milk and the dried cranberries and then spoon the mixture into the prepared cases. Bake in the preheated oven for about 12 minutes or until golden and springy to the touch.

5 I often add a soak to my cupcakes to make them extra moist and scrumptious. While the cupcakes are in the oven, whisk together the icing sugar and orange juice. Remove the cupcakes from the oven and while they are still warm, use a cocktail stick to make a few holes in each cupcake. Pour 2 teaspoons of the orange soak over each cupcake and leave to cool in their tins.

6 Make the buttercream. Put the icing sugar in a bowl with the (very soft) butter, milk and vanilla extract. Beat well, ideally with an electric mixer or an electric hand-held mixer; if you are beating by hand then use a wooden spoon and beat until really fluffy. Fold in the melted white chocolate and beat again.

7 Spread or pipe the buttercream on to the cooled cupcakes and decorate each one with a fresh cranberry or sugar-paste decorations.

TRAY
BAKES

JAMMIEST COCONUT CAKE

I am not sure what it is that I love so much about this cake. Perhaps it is the buttery vanilla sponge speckled with coconut and baked with a layer of sweet raspberry jam. Or the simple layer of icing dredged with desiccated coconut. Or, maybe it is because it just reminds me of being little. I can remember the feel of the desiccated coconut in my fingers and its fragrant, sweetly tropical aroma as I helped to make a similar cake with my mother.

MAKES ABOUT 18 SQUARES	MAKING TIME	BAKING TIME
	20 minutes	35–40 minutes

350 g unsalted butter, softened

350 g caster sugar

6 large eggs

2 tsp vanilla extract

400 g self-raising flour

2 tsp baking powder

170 g desiccated coconut

pinch of salt

8 tbsp raspberry jam

For the topping

200 g icing sugar

2 tbsp boiling water

75 g desiccated coconut

1 Preheat the oven to 180°C (350°F/Gas 4) and line a 20 x 30-cm tray bake tin with non-stick baking paper.

2 Cream together the butter and sugar in an electric mixer. Add the eggs and vanilla extract and beat or whisk well until pale and fluffy.

3 Gently mix in all the dry ingredients. Spoon half of the mixture into the prepared tin and spread out with a palette knife.

4 Dollop the jam on top and spread to evenly cover the mixture. Spoon the remaining mixture on top and spread carefully with a palette knife to cover the jam and create a smooth top.

5 Bake in the preheated oven for about 35–40 minutes or until golden and springy to the touch. Remove the cake from the oven and leave in the tin to cool.

6 Make the topping. Mix together the icing sugar and water, adding the water a little at a time, until you have a smooth, spreadable icing. Roughly spread the icing over the top of the cooled cake then use a spoon to spread the desiccated coconut on top.

7 Leave to set then cut into squares to serve.

This is a great cake to take on holiday or on picnics. It keeps well in an airtight tin or storage container.

MELTING CHOCOLATE HAZELNUT CAKE

A gooey cake, packed with hazelnuts and baked with a secret layer of melting chocolate spread in the middle. This is a super-fast recipe that ticks all the boxes.

MAKES ABOUT 15 PIECES

MAKING TIME
15 minutes

BAKING TIME
35 minutes

200 g unsalted butter, softened

200 g caster sugar

4 large eggs

150 g self-raising flour

50 g cocoa powder

1 tsp baking powder

50 g chopped hazelnuts

2 tbsp semi-skimmed milk

16 tbsp chocolate hazelnut spread, such as Nutella

50 g toasted hazelnuts, roughly chopped, to decorate (optional)

1 Preheat the oven to 180°C (350°F/Gas 4) and line a 20 x 30-cm tray bake tin with non-stick baking paper.

2 Cream together the butter and sugar, add the eggs and whisk until light and fluffy. I do this in an electric mixer fitted with a whisk attachment on a high speed.

3 Add the dry ingredients and mix in gently. Add the milk and stir to combine.

4 Scrape roughly half the mixture into the prepared tin and smooth out.

5 Dollop half the chocolate hazelnut spread on to the cake mix – use a knife to spread over the top of the layer of cake mixture.

6 Spread the rest of the cake mix on top and smooth with a palette knife. Bake in the preheated oven for about 35 minutes, until springy to the touch.

7 Remove from the oven and immediately spoon the remaining chocolate spread on to the hot cake (still in its tin). Leave for about 30 seconds then use a knife to spread it out as it melts to cover the top of the cake. Sprinkle over the chopped toasted hazelnuts, if using.

Miranda's variation

For a delicious twist, replace the hazelnuts with toasted flaked almonds and the chocolate spread with dulce de leche or caramel. Add about 1 teaspoon of sea salt to the caramel too, if you like.

ICED LEMON CURD AND ALMOND BARS

This moist lemon and almond cake is baked with a hidden lemon curd middle, topped with a generous layer of lemon icing, and sliced into elegant bars.

MAKES ABOUT 15 BARS

MAKING TIME
20 minutes

BAKING TIME
25–30 minutes

175 g unsalted butter, softened
175 g caster sugar
3 large eggs
100 g self-raising flour
75 g ground almonds
1 tsp baking powder
grated zest of 2 lemons
4 tbsp lemon curd

For the icing
200 g icing sugar
2 tbsp lemon curd
½ tbsp lemon juice
grated lemon zest and/or
    toasted flaked almonds

1 Preheat the oven to 180°C (350°F/Gas 4) and line a 20 x 30-cm tray bake tin with non-stick baking paper.

2 Put all the ingredients for the cake, except the lemon curd, into a large bowl or the bowl of an electric mixer and beat to combine.

3 Scrape roughly half of the mixture into the prepared tin and spread to cover the base evenly.

4 Dollop on the lemon curd and spread as evenly as possible to create a layer on top of the cake mixture. Scrape the remaining mixture on top and smooth with a palette knife.

5 Bake in the preheated oven for 25–30 minutes or until golden and springy to touch. Remove from the oven and leave to cool in the tin.

6 While the cake is in the oven, make the simple icing by mixing together the icing sugar, lemon curd and lemon juice until smooth. Spread the icing on top of the cooled cake and sprinkle with lemon zest and/or almonds.

To make delightful petit fours, cut the cake into small squares and press a flower decoration on top.

DOUBLE CHOCOLATE SWEETIE CAKE

A thick slab of chocolate cake, studded with chocolate chips, topped with a layer of chocolate buttercream and heaped with chocolate sweets. Great for parties, this recipe is a hit with all ages.

MAKES 15–20 SLICES	MAKING TIME	BAKING TIME
	25 minutes	30–35 minutes

250 g unsalted butter, softened

250 g soft brown sugar

4 large eggs

200 g self-raising flour

50 g cocoa powder

1 tsp baking powder

2 tbsp semi-skimmed milk

1 tsp vanilla extract

200 g milk chocolate drops (or roughly chopped milk chocolate bar)

plenty of chocolate sweets such as Smarties, Minstrels, chopped Crunchie, to decorate

For the icing

175 g plain chocolate

250 g unsalted butter, softened

300 g icing sugar

1 tbsp semi-skimmed milk

1 tsp vanilla extract

1 Preheat the oven to 180°C (350°F/Gas 4) and line a 20 x 30-cm tray bake tin with non-stick baking paper or, if you have it, some foil-lined parchment.

2 Cream together the butter and sugar in an electric mixer. Add the eggs and mix again.

3 Add the flour, cocoa and baking powder and mix gently, then add the milk and vanilla extract and fold in the chocolate drops.

4 Spoon into the prepared tin and smooth with a palette knife. Bake in the preheated oven for 30–35 minutes, or until springy to the touch. Leave to cool in the tin.

5 Make the icing. Melt the chocolate in a bowl in the microwave on high heat for 1 minute. Stir well, then heat again in 30-second bursts until completely melted. Watch carefully as chocolate burns easily in the microwave.

6 Use an electric hand-held mixer or food processor to beat together the butter, icing sugar, milk and vanilla extract. Then add the melted chocolate and beat again on a high speed. Spread the icing over the top of the cooled cake, then cover generously with the chocolate sweeties.

Miranda's variation

To make a Vanilla Sweetie Cake, omit the cocoa powder and increase the self-raising flour to 250 g. Replace the milk chocolate drops with white chocolate drops or roughly chopped white chocolate. Add 1 teaspoon of vanilla extract with the milk. For the icing, replace the plain chocolate with white chocolate. Decorate with white chocolate buttons and brightly coloured sweets.

FUDGY RASPBERRY AND WHITE CHOCOLATE UPSIDE-DOWN CAKE

Topped with a scrumptious layer of caramelised white chocolate ganache, this cake is studded with raspberries and melting white chocolate chunks.

MAKES ABOUT 15 PIECES	MAKING TIME	BAKING TIME
	20 minutes	25 minutes

225 ml double cream
225 g white chocolate
200 g unsalted butter, softened
200 g caster sugar
1 tsp vanilla extract
4 large eggs
350 g self-raising flour
2 tsp baking powder
150 g white chocolate chunks
2 tbsp semi-skimmed milk
150 g raspberries
raspberries and pistachio nuts
   or flaked almonds, to decorate

1 Preheat the oven to 180°C (350°F/Gas 4) and line a 20 x 30-cm tray bake tin with non-stick baking paper.

2 Put the cream and white chocolate in a bowl over a pan of simmering water until the chocolate has just melted, stir to combine then remove from the heat. Pour the chocolate and cream mixture into the prepared tin.

3 Put all the remaining ingredients, except the raspberries, into a large bowl, or the bowl of an electric mixer, and beat until well combined.

4 Spread the cake mixture on top of the ganache layer in the tin and level with a knife. Don't worry if the layers mix a little, this is meant to be homely not perfect. Scatter the raspberries over the top and press into the cake mixture.

5 Bake in the preheated oven for about 25 minutes or until the cake is golden and springy to the touch. Leave to cool in the tin before putting a chopping board or oblong plate over the tin and tipping the cake on to it. The bottom of the cake will now be on the top! Sprinkle with raspberries and toasted flaked almonds or pistachios and serve.

NUTTY FUDGE BARS

These oaty bars are wholesomely nutty, yet extravagantly fudgy – essentially flapjacks dressed in millionaire's clothing.

MAKES ABOUT 15 BARS	MAKING TIME	BAKING TIME
	20 minutes	20–25 minutes

225 g unsalted butter
225 g demerara sugar
2 large egg yolks
1 tsp vanilla extract
115 g plain flour
115 g oats

For the topping
60 g unsalted butter
60 g dark brown sugar
1 x 397-g tin condensed milk
100 g pecan nuts
100 g walnuts
50 g chopped hazelnuts

1 Preheat the oven to 180°C (350°F/Gas 4) and line a 20 x 30-cm tray bake tin with non-stick baking paper.

2 Beat the butter, sugar, egg yolks and vanilla extract together in a bowl with a wooden spoon or in an electric mixer. Add the flour and oats and mix to combine.

3 Press the mixture into the prepared tin and bake in the preheated oven for 20–25 minutes or until the surface looks baked and dry rather than wet.

4 While the base is in the oven, put the butter, sugar and condensed milk for the topping into a pan and bring to the boil, stirring all the time. Simmer gently until it thickens, then remove from the heat and stir in the nuts.

5 Remove the base from the oven and pour the nutty caramel on top. Spread all over with a palette knife then leave to set. Put it in the fridge if you are in a hurry!

6 Use the baking paper to lift the entire tray bake on to a chopping board and then use a large knife to slice into bars.

Miranda's variation

For salty caramel nutty bars add 1 teaspoon of sea salt to the caramel with the nuts.

WHITE CHOCOLATE CHEESECAKE BROWNIE

Creamy white chocolate cheesecake perfectly complements the dark rich chocolate of the brownie. Perfect as it is, or as a pudding with strawberries and cream.

MAKES ABOUT 15 SQUARES	MAKING TIME	BAKING TIME
	20 minutes	35–40 minutes

1 quantity of Best Friend Brownie (see opposite)
350 g full-fat cream cheese
100 g icing sugar
100 g white chocolate, melted
2 large eggs
1 tsp vanilla extract

1 Preheat the oven to 180°C (350°F/Gas 4) and line a 20 x 30-cm tray bake tin with non-stick baking paper or, ideally, with foil-lined baking paper as it is easier to lift out of the tin.

2 Prepare the mix for the Best Friend Brownie (see opposite) and spoon into the prepared tin.

3 Beat all the remaining ingredients together in a bowl with a wooden spoon and spread out on top of the brownie mixture to create as even a layer as possible.

4 Bake in the preheated oven for 35–40 minutes until starting to come away from the sides of the tin. Allow to cool in the tin before cutting into squares.

BEST FRIEND BROWNIE

So called because this versatile recipe will soon be your best friend and you'll not want to be without it!

MAKES ABOUT 15 SQUARES (DEPENDING HOW BIG YOU LIKE YOUR SLICES OF BROWNIE!)	MAKING TIME 15 minutes	BAKING TIME 35–40 minutes

250 g unsalted butter

150 g soft brown sugar

150 g caster sugar

1 tsp vanilla extract

3 large eggs plus 1 egg yolk

200 g plain chocolate, melted in short bursts in the microwave

75 g chocolate drops or chunks (ideally a 70% cocoa solids chocolate)

60 g plain flour

65 g cocoa powder, sifted to remove any lumps

generous pinch of salt (¼ tsp)

½ tsp baking powder

1 Preheat the oven to 180°C (350°F/Gas 4) and line a 20 x 30-cm tray bake tin with non-stick baking paper or, ideally, with foil-lined baking paper as it is easier to lift out of the tin.

2 Using the whisk attachment of an electric mixer, cream together the butter, both sugars and the vanilla extract.

3 Add the eggs and egg yolk and beat furiously for about 3 minutes – this will give a lovely crackly top to the brownie.

4 Fold in the remaining ingredients and scrape into the prepared tin. Bake in the preheated oven for 35–40 minutes. Remove from the oven when the top is flaky and dry and the brownie is springy but not wobbly to the touch. Allow to cool in the tin before cutting.

Miranda's variation

For a salted caramel version of this brownie, mix together 8 tablespoons of dulce de leche (I use Nestlé Carnation Caramel) and 1 teaspoon of sea salt flakes. Dollop on to the brownie mixture and swirl through the mixture before baking in the oven as above.

To keep your brownie super squidgy, remove the tin from the oven, place it on a heatproof board or chopping board and put the whole thing straight into the fridge!

SALTY DOG BROWNIE

Friendly, bouncy and smothering you with love like a dog rushing up the beach and covering you with seawater! Gorgeous salted caramel is rippled through the brownie and a salted chocolate chip cookie dough is baked into the top. I often omit the salt if making this for my children.

MAKES 12 GENEROUS SQUARES (OR MORE IF CUT CONSERVATIVELY!)	MAKING TIME 25 minutes	BAKING TIME 35 minutes

1 quantity of Best Friend Brownie (see page 77)

8 tbsp dulce de leche (I use Nestlé Carnation Caramel)

1 tsp sea salt flakes

For the topping

110 g unsalted butter, softened

175 g light soft brown sugar

1 tsp vanilla extract

1 large egg

200 g plain flour

1 tsp sea salt flakes

1 tsp bicarbonate of soda

100 g milk chocolate chunks

1 Preheat the oven to 180°C (350°F/Gas 4) and line a 20 x 30-cm tray bake tin with non-stick baking paper or, ideally, with foil-lined baking paper as it is easier to lift out of the tin.

2 Prepare the mixture for the Best Friend Brownie (see page 77) and spoon into the prepared tin.

3 Mix together the dulce de leche and sea salt flakes and dollop on top of the brownie mix. Use a palette knife to swirl into the mixture and then bake in the preheated oven for about 15 minutes while you make the topping.

4 Put all the topping ingredients except the chocolate chunks into a large bowl and mix together well with a wooden spoon. Stir in the chocolate chunks.

5 Remove the brownie after 15 minutes and then crumble the topping over the top. Return to the oven and bake for a further 20 minutes. Allow to cool a little in the tin before slicing into generous squares and devouring.

AUTUMN PUMPKIN CAKE

Rustic, homely and full of good things.

MAKES ABOUT 15 SQUARES	MAKING TIME	BAKING TIME
	20 minutes	50 minutes

400 g plain flour

1½ tsp baking powder

1 tsp mixed spice

½ tsp salt

450 g soft brown sugar

3 large eggs, lightly beaten

185 ml sunflower oil

225 g peeled, deseeded and grated pumpkin (use butternut squash instead, if you prefer)

135 ml orange juice

For the topping

200 g full-fat cream cheese

3 tbsp icing sugar

2 tsp grated orange zest

50 g toasted flaked almonds

2 tbsp clear honey

1 Preheat the oven to 170°C (325°F/Gas 3) and line a 20 x 30-cm tray bake tin with non-stick baking paper.

2 Put all the ingredients for the cake into a large mixing bowl and mix together until well combined.

3 Spoon into the prepared tin and bake in the preheated oven for about 50 minutes, until springy to the touch and coming away from the sides of the tin. Leave to cool in the tin.

4 While the cake is cooking, use a spoon to mix together the cream cheese, icing sugar and orange zest. Generously spread this on top of the cooled cake. Sprinkle with the almonds and drizzle with honey.

STICKY GINGERBREAD
WITH THICK LEMON ICING

This is one of the most comforting cakes to bake. I only have to be reminded of the taste, and I am rushing to the kitchen to put one in the oven! Great for rainy days and for taking on windy walks. This cake is quick and simple to make, lasts well in the tin and is hard to beat!

MAKES ABOUT 15 SQUARES	MAKING TIME	BAKING TIME
	15 minutes	35 minutes

125 g unsalted butter
130 g dark brown sugar
2 tbsp treacle
200 g golden syrup
250 g self-raising flour
3 tsp ground ginger
½ tsp mixed spice
1 tsp bicarbonate of soda
pinch of salt
2 large eggs
240 ml semi-skimmed milk

For the icing
500 g icing sugar
juice of 1 lemon (about 8 tbsp)

1 Preheat the oven to 180°C (350°F/Gas 4) and line a 20 x 30-cm tray bake tin with non-stick baking paper.

2 Melt the butter, sugar, treacle and golden syrup in a small pan over a low heat.

3 Put all the dry ingredients into a large mixing bowl and stir together with a wooden spoon to combine. Add the melted butter and syrup mixture and stir again.

4 Mix together the eggs and milk in a jug and add to the mixture. Stir until you have a sloppy batter. Pour into the prepared tin and bake in the preheated oven for about 35 minutes.

5 Remove from the oven when the cake is springy to touch and coming away from the sides of the tin. Leave in the tin to cool completely.

6 Put the icing sugar into a large bowl and stir in the lemon juice to make a thick icing. When the cake is completely cold, spread a thick layer of icing over the top and leave to set. Once the icing has set, use a large sharp knife to cut into squares.

CRUNCHIE

My Great Auntie Ethel was a school cook in the 1940s. She used to make this for the children at the village school in Chapel-en-le-Frith and often for my mother when she was a little girl. It is one of the first recipes I can remember making as a child and I still use the recipe book where it is written in my six-year-old handwriting.

MAKES ABOUT 15 SQUARES	MAKING TIME	BAKING TIME
	10 minutes	20–25 minutes

255 g unsalted butter

165 g sugar

3 tbsp syrup

125 g oats

125 g cornflakes

100 g chocolate drops (milk or plain)

1 Preheat the oven to 180°C (350°F/Gas 4) and line a 20 x 30-cm tray bake tin with non-stick baking paper or, ideally, with foil-lined baking paper.

2 Put the butter, sugar and syrup in a saucepan, melt over a low heat and stir to combine. Stir in the oats and cornflakes.

3 Press the mixture into the prepared tin and bake in the preheated oven for 15–20 minutes. Remove from the oven, sprinkle the chocolate drops on top and return to the oven for a further 3–5 minutes.

4 Remove from the oven and spread the chocolate over the top with a knife. Leave to cool and for the chocolate to harden (I usually put it in the fridge to speed things up) then slice into squares or bars.

APRICOT, SULTANA AND PECAN BARS

Sweet and delicious yet wholesome and fruity, these bars have a light layer of brown-sugar sponge packed with oats, apricots, sultanas and pecans and topped with a sticky layer of apricot jam and even more nuts. This is a quick, all-in-one cake that's delicious eaten warm, making it the perfect last-minute bake.

MAKES ABOUT 18 BARS

MAKING TIME
20 minutes

BAKING TIME
20–25 minutes

200 g unsalted butter, softened

200 g soft brown sugar

2 tbsp clear honey

3 large eggs

1 tsp vanilla extract

150 g self-raising flour

1 tsp baking powder

50 g oats

¼ tsp salt

1 tbsp apricot jam

120 g dried apricots, chopped

70 g sultanas

100 g pecan nuts

For the topping

200 g apricot jam

2 tbsp water

200 g pecan nuts

1 Preheat the oven to 180°C (350°F/Gas 4) and line a 20 x 30-cm tray bake tin with non-stick baking paper.

2 Cream together the butter, sugar and honey in a large bowl or in an electric mixer. Beat in the eggs one at a time, and then mix in all the remaining ingredients.

3 Spoon the mixture into the prepared tin and bake in the preheated oven for 20–25 minutes until golden and springy to the touch.

4 Just before the cake is ready to come out of the oven, make the topping. Put the apricot jam and water in a small pan and bring to the boil. Bubble gently for about a minute.

5 Remove the cake from the oven and, while it is still in the tin, scatter over the pecans and then pour over the warm apricot glaze. Leave to cool in the tin before slicing into bars.

GINGER FLAPJACKS

One of my daughter Eleanor's friends, Florrie, gave us this recipe, and we call these Florrie's flapjacks. Her granny is only allowed to come and stay if she brings a box of these with her as her passport! Gingery flapjack is topped with a layer of warming syrupy gingered icing. Wholesome and utterly addictive.

MAKES ABOUT 15 SLICES	MAKING TIME	BAKING TIME
	15 minutes	20 minutes

225 g unsalted butter
225 g soft brown sugar
4 tsp ground ginger
4 tsp golden syrup
450 g oats

For the icing
170 g unsalted butter
100 g icing sugar
2 tsp ground ginger
6 tsp golden syrup

1 Preheat the oven to 160°C (320°F/Gas 2–3) and line a 20 x 30-cm tray bake tin with non-stick baking paper.

2 Put the butter, sugar, ground ginger and syrup into a pan and melt over a low heat. Stir in the oats.

3 Press into the prepared tin and bake in the preheated oven for 20 minutes until evenly golden and with the same texture across the top – take care not to over bake.

4 Put the butter, icing sugar, ground ginger and syrup in a small pan and melt gently. Mix in the icing sugar and stir to combine.

5 Remove the flapjack from the oven and leave in the tin to cool before spreading with the icing. Leave to set.

BUTTERY VANILLA AND BERRY CRUNCH BARS

Buttery vanilla sponge cake, heaped with summer berries and baked with a meltingly good layer of crumbled shortbread. Keep frozen berries in the freezer so you can make this at the drop of a hat.

MAKES ABOUT 15 BARS	MAKING TIME	BAKING TIME
	20 minutes	25 minutes

200 g unsalted butter, softened

175 g caster sugar

2 large eggs

1 tsp vanilla extract

75 g ground almonds

125 g self-raising flour

200 g berries (I use frozen mixed berries)

For the shortbread topping

80 g self-raising flour

40 g chilled unsalted butter, diced

50 g light soft brown sugar

1 Preheat the oven to 180°C (350°F/Gas 4) and line a 20 x 30-cm tray bake tin with non-stick baking paper.

2 First make the shortbread topping. Whizz together the flour, butter and sugar in the food processor or rub together with your fingertips until the mixture resembles rough breadcrumbs. Set aside.

3 Whisk together the butter, sugar, eggs and vanilla extract in an electric mixer. Gently mix in the ground almonds and flour.

4 Scrape into the prepared tin and place in the preheated oven. After 10 minutes, remove the cake from the oven and sprinkle the frozen berries on top.

5 Roughly spread the shortbread mixture over the top and return to the oven to bake for a further 15 minutes until the crumble topping is golden and crisp.

6 Leave to cool in the tin before cutting into portions. Alternatively, serve while still warm with ice cream for a delicious pudding.

BANOFFEE BLONDIES

Another excuse to enjoy the much-loved combination of banana and toffee. This recipe is lovely on its own, but also makes a quick and easy pudding that's delicious with vanilla ice cream.

MAKES 15 SQUARES	MAKING TIME	BAKING TIME
	20 minutes	30–35 minutes

180 g white chocolate (150 g for melting and 30 g broken into chunks for sprinkling)

150 g unsalted butter, softened

250 g light soft brown sugar

1 tsp vanilla extract

3 large eggs plus 1 egg yolk

150 g plain flour

50 g digestive biscuits, broken into pieces

2 bananas, sliced

8 tbsp dulce de leche (I use Nestlé Carnation Caramel)

100 g fudge pieces

1 Preheat the oven to 180°C (350°F/Gas 4) and line a 20 x 30-cm tray bake tin with non-stick baking paper or, ideally, with foil-lined baking paper.

2 Melt the 150 g white chocolate in a bowl over a pan of simmering water; alternatively melt it in a microwave in short bursts, taking care not to let it burn.

3 Cream together the butter, sugar and vanilla in an electric mixer, then beat in the eggs and egg yolk at high speed. If making by hand, whisk furiously with a balloon whisk.

4 Fold in the flour, melted white chocolate, biscuit chunks and the sliced bananas. Scrape into the prepared tin and dollop the dulce de leche on top, then swirl into the mixture with a knife.

5 Sprinkle the white chocolate chunks and fudge pieces on top before putting into the oven to bake for 30–35 minutes until evenly golden, the surface looks dry and the blondie is coming away from the sides of the tin. Allow to cool in the tin before slicing into squares.

GOODNESS BARS

These bars are packed with goodness from the bananas, apricots, dates, seeds, dried fruit and oats, and are great to make when you want to use up bits from the storecupboard. Super-quick and easy to make, they are great for energy boosts, nourishing snacks and breakfast on the run!

MAKES ABOUT 18 BARS	MAKING TIME	BAKING TIME
	10 minutes	20-25 minutes

100 g unsalted butter

3 tbsp golden syrup

25 g desiccated coconut

25 g mixed seeds, such as pumpkin and sunflower

30 g dates, chopped

55 g dried apricots, chopped

100 g dried fruits, such as sultanas, currants, raisins

2 bananas, mashed

100 g oats

100 g rice crispies

2 tbsp golden linseed, to sprinkle on top

1 Preheat the oven to 180°C (350°F/Gas 4) and line a 20 x 30-cm tray bake tin with non-stick baking paper.

2 Melt the butter and syrup in a pan and set aside.

3 Put all the remaining ingredients, except the linseed, into a large mixing bowl, stir in the melted butter and syrup and mix well to combine.

4 Scrape the mixture into the prepared tin. Press down well with the back of a spoon and then sprinkle with the linseed or some more mixed seeds.

5 Bake in the preheated oven for about 20–25 minutes or until golden and starting to crisp around the edges of the tin.

Drizzle with 100 g of good-quality melted chocolate (70% cocoa solids) once cooled – if you dare.

CRUNCHY BROWN SUGAR DATE CAKE

Apparently, this was the Queen Mother's favourite cake. It is packed with dates and crunchy walnuts, and the brown sugar crust is its crowning glory. This recipe was given to my husband's grandmother 'on good authority' many years ago.

MAKES ABOUT 15 PIECES	MAKING TIME	BAKING TIME
	15 minutes	35 minutes

225 g chopped dates
250 ml boiling water
1 tsp bicarbonate of soda
225 g granulated sugar
1 large egg, beaten
285 g plain flour
½ tsp salt
85 g unsalted butter, melted
1 tsp vanilla extract
1 tsp baking powder
55 g chopped walnuts

For the topping
5 tbsp brown sugar
2 tbsp unsalted butter
2 tbsp semi-skimmed milk

1 Preheat the oven to 190°C (375°F/Gas 5) and line a 20 x 30-cm tray bake tin with non-stick baking paper.

2 Put the dates in a bowl, pour over the boiling water then add the bicarbonate of soda and stir to combine. Put to one side.

3 Put all the remaining cake ingredients in the bowl of an electric mixer and mix together well; alternatively use a large bowl and wooden spoon. Add the date mixture and stir to combine.

4 Scrape into the prepared tin and level with a palette knife. Bake in the preheated oven for about 35 minutes or until the cake is golden and springy to the touch.

5 Put the ingredients for the topping in a small pan and bubble for about 3 minutes. Remove the cake from the oven and pour the topping over the top. Leave to cool in the tin before slicing into squares.

CHRISTMAS TRAY BAKE

Crisp pastry, mincemeat, cranberries and thick frangipane, sprinkled with flaked almonds. A super-quick and meltingly good alternative to mince pies.

MAKES AT LEAST 15 PIECES	MAKING TIME 20 minutes	BAKING TIME 35 minutes

For the pastry (or see Miranda's tip, below)

175 g plain flour

85 g unsalted butter

25 g icing sugar

1 large egg

For the frangipane

255 g unsalted butter, softened

255 g caster sugar

4 large eggs, beaten

50 g plain flour, sifted

255 g ground almonds

1 jar of good-quality mincemeat

150 g dried cranberries

For the topping

50 g flaked almonds

1 Preheat the oven to 180°C (350°F/Gas 4) and line a 20 x 30-cm tray bake tin with non-stick baking paper.

2 To make the pastry, put the flour, butter and icing sugar in a food processor and whizz until you have a crumbly mixture. Add the egg and mix again until you have a soft/crumbly dough. Pull together with your hands then roll out on a lightly floured surface into a rough rectangle to fit the base of the tin.

3 Press the dough into the prepared tin in an even layer and blind bake: put a sheet of baking paper on top of the pastry and tip in baking beans in a single layer. Bake in the preheated oven for 10 minutes, then remove the beans and paper and return to the oven for a further 5 minutes.

4 For the topping, cream together the butter and sugar in an electric mixer at high speed until pale. Add the eggs and beat gently until well incorporated. Fold in the flour and ground almonds to make frangipane.

5 Spread the mincemeat on to the pastry base and sprinkle with the cranberries. Spread the frangipane on top, sprinkle with the flaked almonds and then bake in the preheated oven for 20 minutes, or until the top is light golden and springy to the touch. Allow to cool in the tin.

For an even quicker version, use ready-made shortcrust pastry (ready rolled is even better) instead of making your own. Use to line your prepared tin and blind bake as above.

LOAF CAKES

PLUM BREAD IN A HURRY

Lincolnshire plum bread is a rich, yeast-based loaf, traditionally made at Christmas with dried fruit. Packed with prunes that have been soaked in apple juice to rejuvenate their plumminess, this is my speedy twist on an old recipe. This is delicious eaten warm, thickly spread with butter!

MAKES ONE 2-LB LOAF	MAKING TIME	BAKING TIME
	5 minutes	35 minutes

250 g prunes, roughly chopped

160 ml apple juice

1 large egg

225 g self-raising flour

150 g soft brown sugar

1 tsp mixed spice

pinch of salt

1 tbsp demerara sugar, for sprinkling

1 Preheat the oven to 180°C (350°F/Gas 4) and line a 2-lb loaf tin with non-stick baking paper or use a loaf tin liner.

2 Put the chopped prunes (I chop each prune into roughly 3 slices) in a large bowl and pour over the apple juice. Heat in the microwave for 1 minute on high or in a small pan over a medium heat.

3 Remove the bowl from the microwave, add all the remaining ingredients, except the demerara sugar, and stir well to combine.

4 Scrape the mixture into the prepared tin, sprinkle over the demerara sugar and bake in the preheated oven for about 35 minutes, or until a skewer inserted into the centre comes out clean. Leave to cool in the tin.

RAISIN BREAD

This raisin bread is the stuff nursery teas are made of. If you want to recreate a storybook world in your kitchen in a jiffy, this is the recipe for you. It will probably be eaten in one sitting, but any leftovers can be used to make scrumptious toast.

MAKES ONE 2-LB LOAF	MAKING TIME	BAKING TIME
	10 minutes	45 minutes

340 g self-raising flour
½ tsp salt
85 g caster sugar
100 g raisins
2 large eggs
265 ml semi-skimmed milk
55 g unsalted butter

1 Preheat the oven to 180°C (350°F/Gas 4) and line a 2-lb loaf tin with non-stick baking paper or use a loaf tin liner.

2 Sift the flour, salt and sugar into a large bowl and then stir in the raisins.

3 Break the eggs into a jug and mix in the milk with a fork. Melt the butter in a small pan or gently in the microwave and add to the milk and egg mixture. Mix into the dry ingredients with a wooden spoon.

4 Scrape into the prepared tin and bake in the middle or bottom of the preheated oven for 45 minutes or until a skewer comes out clean. Leave to cool in the tin for at least 10 minutes before turning out on to a wire rack. Either leave to cool completely or eat straight away!

BROWN SUGAR AND APPLE SPICED LOAF

My husband calls this cake 'gingery bread pudding'. It is something I often make with the windfall apples in our garden. Delicious on its own, or smothered in custard or ice cream.

MAKES ONE 2-LB LOAF	MAKING TIME	BAKING TIME
	15 minutes	1 hour to bake

300 g cooking apples,
  such as Bramley

grated zest and juice
  of 1 lemon

225 g unsalted butter

225 g soft brown sugar

3 large eggs

225 g self-raising flour

2 tsp baking powder

1 tsp ground ginger

1 tsp mixed spice

25 g ground almonds

1 tbsp demerara sugar, to
  sprinkle

1 Preheat the oven to 180°C (350°F/Gas 4) and line a 2-lb loaf tin with non-stick baking paper or use a loaf tin liner.

2 Peel, core and chop the apples into 1-cm dice. Place in a bowl and toss with the lemon juice to prevent discolouring.

3 Cream the butter, sugar and lemon zest by hand in a large bowl or in an electric mixer. Add the eggs and beat well to combine.

4 Sift together the flour, baking powder and spices and fold into the mixture with the ground almonds.

5 Drain the apple pieces and stir into the mixture, then spoon into the prepared tin. Bake in the preheated oven for 1 hour, or until dark golden and coming away from the sides of the tin.

6 As soon as the cake comes out of the oven, sprinkle with the demerara sugar and leave to cool in the tin.

CLEMENTINE, PISTACHIO AND HONEY LOAF

The sweetest clementine cake, drizzled with honey and crowned with a crumble of toasted green pistachio nuts. This is delicious eaten while still warm.

MAKES ONE 2-LB LOAF	MAKING TIME	BAKING TIME
	15 minutes	40 minutes

175 g unsalted butter, softened

175 g caster sugar

3 large eggs

1 tsp vanilla extract

2 clementines (or 1 orange)

175 g self-raising flour

50 g ground almonds

2 tbsp lemon juice

2 tbsp clear honey

50 g pistachio nuts,
   roughly chopped

For the topping

50 g pistachio nuts,
   roughly chopped

100 g clear honey

1 tbsp lemon or orange juice

1 Preheat the oven to 180°C (350°F/Gas 4) and line a 2-lb loaf tin with non-stick baking paper or use a loaf tin liner to save time.

2 Cream together the butter and sugar and then beat in the eggs and vanilla extract until the mixture is light and fluffy.

3 Use a coarse grater to grate the whole clementines or orange (skin, pith and flesh) straight into the mixture. Add the, flour, ground almonds and lemon juice and mix gently until combined.

4 Fold the honey into the mixture with the pistachio nuts. Spoon into the prepared tin and bake on a low shelf in the preheated oven for about 40 minutes or until the cake is golden and springy to the touch.

5 Prepare the topping. Toast the pistachio nuts in a dry frying pan for about 4 minutes. Warm the honey and lemon or orange juice in the microwave.

6 As soon as the cake comes out of the oven, pour over the honey and juice mixture, sprinkle with the toasted nuts and leave to cool in the tin.

For a lovely pudding, bake in a 20-cm round loose-bottomed tin and serve with a bowl of thick Greek yoghurt.

COFFEE STREUSEL LOAF

The nutty, crumbly streusel topping is added to the cake during baking, making this a speedy cake that is ready to enjoy as soon as it comes out of the oven.

MAKES ONE 2-LB LOAF	MAKING TIME	BAKING TIME
	10 minutes	30–35 minutes

175 g unsalted butter, softened

175 g soft brown light sugar

3 large eggs

175 g self-raising flour

1 tsp baking powder

1 tbsp instant coffee mixed
 with 1 tsp boiling water

For the streusel

100 g nuts (walnuts, hazelnuts
 and toasted almonds)

1 tbsp plain flour

100 g soft light brown sugar

50 g cold butter, diced

1 Preheat the oven to 180°C (350°F/Gas 4) and line a 2-lb loaf tin with non-stick baking paper or use a loaf tin liner.

2 Put all the ingredients for the streusel in a food processor and whizz briefly; alternatively, rub together with your fingers, rather like making a simple crumble. Set aside.

3 Put all the cake ingredients into a bowl and beat well with a wooden spoon; alternatively mix in an electric mixer.

4 Scrape the cake mixture into the prepared tin and bake in the preheated oven for about 15 minutes. Remove from the oven, spread the streusel on top and return to the oven for a further 15–20 minutes, or until a skewer comes out clean. Leave to cool in the tin for at least 10 minutes before serving warm or transferring to a wire rack to cool completely.

CRUNCHY-TOPPED BARA BRITH (WELSH TEA BREAD)

We have spent many happy family holidays at my mother-in-law's house in Wales. One of our favourite things has been returning from wet walks to devour thick slices of warm bara brith, spread with lashings of farmhouse butter, while we warm our toes in front of the wood-burner. Instead of orange zest, this recipe uses marmalade, an ingredient used often in baking during the war when fresh fruit was not readily available. It makes the recipe even quicker to make.

MAKES ONE 2-LB LOAF

MAKING TIME
10 minutes

BAKING TIME
1–1¼ hours

450 g dried fruit (I use sultanas and currants but any dried fruit will do)

300 ml cold tea, made with 4 tea bags and 300 ml boiling water

450 g self-raising flour

1 tsp mixed spice

175 g soft brown sugar

1 large egg, lightly beaten

2 tbsp marmalade

50 g crunchy sugar, such as demerara or granulated, pearlsocker or pearl sugar

1 Preheat the oven to 180°C (350°F/Gas 4). Butter a 2-lb loaf tin or 18-cm cake tin and dust with flour or use a loaf tin liner.

2 Put the dried fruit into a bowl and pour over the tea. Leave to soak while you get on with weighing out the remaining ingredients. You can also soak the fruit overnight if you don't want to make the bara brith straight away.

3 Put all the remaining ingredients, except the crunchy sugar, into a large mixing bowl then pour in the dried fruit and all the soaking liquid. Stir with a wooden spoon until well combined and add a few tablespoons of water (or milk) if the mixture is a little dry.

4 Scrape the sticky mixture into the prepared tin and then cover the top with crunchy sugar. Bake in the bottom or middle of the preheated oven for about 1 hour.

5 Check whether the bara brith is done by inserting a skewer or sharp knife into the centre; it should come out clean. If the knife is sticky return to the oven for a further 10 minutes and test again. Leave to cool in the tin for at least 15 minutes before tipping onto a wire rack. Best eaten warm.

DARK CHOCOLATE AND COURGETTE LOAF WITH FUDGE ICING

Dark, chocolatey and with the texture of the moistest fudge cake, this tastes sinfully good but its naughtiness is just an act. It is vegan (without the chocolate decorations), contributes to your 'five a day' and, as cakes go, is almost good for you.

MAKES ONE 2-LB LOAF	MAKING TIME	BAKING TIME
	15 minutes	40–45 minutes

200 g plain flour
200 g caster sugar
80 g cocoa powder
1 tsp bicarbonate of soda
½ tsp salt
5 tbsp vegetable oil
1 tsp vinegar (white wine or malt vinegar)
1 tsp vanilla extract
250 ml water
150 g raw courgettes, grated

For the icing
35 g margarine
2 tbsp cocoa powder
2 tbsp boiling water
180 g icing sugar

1 Preheat the oven to 180°C (350°F/Gas 4) and line a 2-lb loaf tin with non-stick baking paper or use a loaf tin liner.

2 Sift all the dry ingredients into a large bowl or whizz in a food processor to combine.

3 Add the oil, vinegar, vanilla and water and mix well until everything is combined. Stir in the grated courgettes.

4 Scrape into the prepared tin and bake in the preheated oven for about 40–45 minutes, or until a skewer comes out clean. Leave to cool in the tin.

5 To make the icing place the dairy-free margarine, cocoa powder and water in a bowl and melt gently in the microwave or in a small pan over a low heat. Stir in the icing sugar and mix well until smooth. Spread a generous layer on the top of the cooled cake.

Miranda's variations

For a delicious finishing touch, cover the iced cake generously with grated chocolate 70% cocoa solids.

For a pretty touch, I decorate the loaf with a few edible flowers (see page 104). Crystallised flowers also look lovely (see page 9). If giving as a gift, pop the loaf into a fresh loaf liner, a cellophane bag or cake box and tie with a contrasting ribbon.

For parties or a simple Christmas decoration, push ready-made decorations, such as chocolate stars, into the icing (see page 105).

FIVE-MINUTE STICKY MALT LOAF

My children have great fun timing me making this and can never believe malt loaf can be made so quickly. It is the fastest recipe possible, and is usually gobbled up in less time than it takes to make.

MAKES ONE 2-LB LOAF	MAKING TIME	BAKING TIME
	5 minutes	45 minutes

325 g self-raising flour

175 g dark brown sugar

pinch of salt

250 g raisins

1 tbsp black treacle

250 ml semi-skimmed milk

3 tbsp clear honey, to glaze

1 Preheat the oven to 180°C (350°F/Gas 4) and line a 2-lb loaf tin with non-stick baking paper or use a loaf tin liner.

2 Put the flour, sugar, salt and fruit into a large bowl. Stir to combine – you may need to crush the sugar a little with the back of a spoon.

3 To measure out your treacle, dip a tablespoon into the flour, then put it straight into the treacle. Spoon the treacle into a measuring jug and then add the milk to the jug. Put the milk and treacle into the microwave to warm for about 1 minute. Stir well then pour on to the dry ingredients. Mix well with a wooden spoon.

4 Spoon the mixture into the prepared tin and bake in the preheated oven for about 45 minutes or until the cake is golden and springy to the touch. Remove from the oven and immediately spoon the honey over the top. Leave to cool in the tin for about 15 minutes before turning out on to a rack to cool completely. Slice and spread with butter.

NOTE

In case you are wondering ... the last time I made this I completed it in 4 minutes 36 seconds.

BLUSTERY BANANA BREAD

Banana bread for a blustery walk on the beach! I have tried lots of recipes for banana bread and, after many tweaks and changes, I think this is a lovely light-tasting loaf with just the right level of sweetness. It can be eaten as a cake, or in thick slices spread with butter. We love to go to the beach (whatever the weather) and take this with us – wrapped in tin foil and accompanied by a flask of hot chocolate.

MAKES ONE 2-LB LOAF	MAKING TIME	BAKING TIME
	10 minutes	35 minutes

80 g unsalted butter, softened

170 g soft light brown sugar

2 large eggs

185 g self-raising flour

½ tsp salt

1 tsp baking powder

350 g bananas, 1 sliced and the remainder mashed

1 Preheat the oven to 180°C (350°F/Gas 4) and line a 2-lb loaf tin with non-stick baking paper or use a loaf tin liner.

2 Put the butter and sugar into the bowl of an electric mixer fitted with a whisk attachment and beat together; alternatively beat furiously by hand with a balloon whisk.

3 Add the eggs and whisk at a high speed for 3 minutes. Use a spoon to fold in the flour, salt and baking powder, then stir in the mashed bananas. Add the sliced bananas at the end.

4 Scrape into the prepared tin and bake in the preheated oven for about 35 minutes, until a skewer comes out clean. Leave to cool in the tin.

Here are some extras that I love to add to this cake: 100 g sultanas, 100 g milk chocolate chunks, 1 tsp ground cinnamon or 100 g dark chocolate chips.

GOLDEN FRUIT LOAF

A comforting loaf, packed with fruit and rich with the flavour of golden syrup. This is a useful recipe to bake if you've run out of eggs!

MAKES ONE 2-LB LOAF	MAKING TIME	BAKING TIME
	15 minutes	1 hour

85 g margarine

110 g caster sugar

85 g golden syrup

280 g self-raising flour (you could also use gluten-free flour)

1½ tsp bicarbonate of soda

½ tsp salt

2 tsp grated orange zest (optional)

250 g fruit (I use roughly 50 g glacé cherries, 100 g chopped dried apricots and 100 g sultanas)

250 ml semi-skimmed milk (you could also use rice milk to make this dairy free)

For the icing (optional)

100 g icing sugar

2–3 tsp orange juice

1 Preheat the oven to 150°C (300°F/Gas 2) and line a 2-lb loaf tin with non-stick baking paper or use a loaf tin liner to save time.

2 Put the margarine, sugar and syrup into a pan and melt over a low heat.

3 Put the flour, bicarbonate of soda, salt, orange zest and fruit in a large bowl and stir to combine. Add the melted margarine, sugar and syrup mixture and the milk and stir together with a wooden spoon.

4 Scrape the mixture into the prepared tin and bake in the preheated oven for about 1 hour, or until a knife inserted into the centre comes out clean. Cool on a wire rack.

5 If you want to ice the cake, mix together the icing sugar and orange juice until smooth. Spread over the top of the cooled cake before serving.

LEMON LOAF CAKE WITH
ZESTY BUTTER ICING

I adore lemons and love to inhale their wonderful invigorating smell when I make this cake. Extra zest is added to the buttercream to create even more flavour. Lemonaholics be warned!

MAKES ONE 2-LB LOAF	MAKING TIME	BAKING TIME
	10 minutes	25–30 minutes

200 g unsalted butter, softened
200 g caster sugar
grated zest of 2 large lemons
3 large eggs, lightly beaten
225 g self-raising flour
1 tsp baking powder
2–3 tbsp lemon juice

For the butter icing
200 g icing sugar
50 g unsalted butter, softened
juice of 1 lemon
2 tsp grated lemon zest

1 Preheat the oven to 180°C (350°F/Gas 4) and line a 2-lb loaf tin with non-stick baking paper or use a loaf tin liner.

2 Put all the cake ingredients into the bowl of an electric mixer and beat well to combine.

3 Scrape into the prepared tin, smooth the top and bake in the preheated oven for about 25 minutes, or until a skewer inserted in the centre comes out clean.

4 While the cake is in the oven, make the butter icing. Mix together the icing sugar, butter, lemon juice and zest; you can do this in a food processor or by hand with a fork.

5 Leave the cake to cool in the tin before spreading with the butter icing.

PUDDING
CAKES

MILK CHOCOLATE
HONEYCOMB TRUFFLE CAKE

This stunning cake keeps two secrets. The first is a melting layer of golden honeycomb baked in its chocolatey heart. The second is a gooey baked chocolate ganache, hidden at the bottom during its baking to create a wonderful rich topping when the cake is turned upside down to serve.

SERVES 6	MAKING TIME	BAKING TIME
	20 minutes	25 minutes

100 g unsalted butter, softened

100 g caster sugar

2 large eggs

150 g self-raising flour

25 g cocoa powder, plus
  extra for dusting

1 tsp baking powder

100 g milk chocolate, melted

1 tbsp semi-skimmed milk

4 honeycomb bars (I use Crunchie bars)

For the ganache

150 ml double cream

150 g milk chocolate

1 Preheat the oven to 180°C (350°F/Gas 4). Line a 20-cm round cake tin with non-stick baking paper or a cake tin liner. If you are not using a liner place the tin on a baking sheet to catch any spillages. Dust the base of the lined tin with cocoa powder.

2 Put the cream and chocolate for the ganache in a bowl over a pan of simmering water, stir to combine then remove from the heat. Pour the chocolate and cream mixture into the tin.

3 Put all the remaining ingredients, except the honeycomb bars, into a large bowl, or the bowl of an electric mixer, and beat well until combined.

4 Smash up the honeycomb bars and spread about one-third on top of the chocolate and cream mixture in the tin.

5 Spread the cake mixture on top and level with a knife. Don't worry if the layers mix a little, this is meant to be homely not perfect. Bake in the preheated oven for about 25 minutes until springy to the touch.

6 Remove from the oven and leave to cool in the tin. Put a plate over the tin and tip the cake on to it. The bottom of the cake will now be on the top! Sprinkle with the remaining crushed honeycomb bars and serve.

SWEET ORANGE TOSCA CAKE

Tosca cake is a much-loved favourite across Scandinavia. In this version a moist and light sponge cake, flavoured with orange, is topped with crisp, caramelized almonds. The praline-like topping and sweet orange combine to make a heavenly cake. A simple yet stunning pudding that always meets with approval.

SERVES 6–8	MAKING TIME	BAKING TIME
	20 minutes	40 minutes

140 g unsalted butter

2 large eggs

170 g caster sugar

125 g plain flour

1 tsp baking powder

grated zest of 1 large orange

2 tbsp orange juice

For the topping

70 g unsalted butter

125 g flaked almonds

3 tbsp caster sugar

1 tbsp plain flour

1 tbsp orange juice

1 Preheat the oven to 180°C (350°F/Gas 4) and line a 20-cm round loose-bottomed cake tin with non-stick baking paper or a cake tin liner.

2 Melt the butter in a small pan or gently in the microwave and put to one side to cool a little.

3 Whisk together the eggs and sugar in an electric mixer until fluffy and thick – this will take about 3 minutes.

4 Sift in the flour and baking powder and mix in gently on a low speed, or fold in with a metal spoon. Mix in the melted butter, orange zest and orange juice.

5 Spoon into the prepared tin, spread to level the top and bake in the preheated oven for 20 minutes.

6 While the cake is in the oven, put all the topping ingredients in a small pan and cook until just bubbling. Once the cake has been in the oven for 20 minutes, remove the cake, pour the topping over the top and return to the oven to bake for a further 10–15 minutes, or until golden brown on top.

7 Remove from the oven and leave the cake to cool in the tin.

APPLE AMBER CAKE

Apple amber is the name given to a traditional farmhouse pudding in Ireland, rather like an apple meringue pie. As soon as I discovered this wonderful confection, I was rushing to create a cake version. Here the crisp meringue, with its marshmallow sweetness, combines with a zesty lemon cake and sharp, lemony apple curd.

SERVES 6–8	MAKING TIME	BAKING TIME
	25 minutes	35 minutes

50 g unsalted butter

125 g caster sugar

1 tsp vanilla extract

2 large egg yolks

125 g self-raising flour

1 tsp baking powder

4 tbsp semi-skimmed milk

grated zest of 1 lemon

For the filling

2 cooking apples, peeled
  and coarsely grated

100 g caster sugar

juice of ½ lemon

2 large egg yolks

For the meringue

4 large egg whites

225 g caster sugar

1 Preheat the oven to 180°C (350°F/Gas 4) and line an 18–20-cm round springform cake tin with non-stick baking paper. The paper should sit about 3 cm above the top of the tin.

2 First prepare the filling. Put the grated apples into a pan, add about 2 tablespoons of water and cook over a medium heat, stirring all the time. Remove from the heat as soon as the apple has become mainly purée. Stir in the sugar and lemon juice, then add the egg yolks and beat well. Set aside.

3 Whisk together the butter and sugar in an electric mixer at a high speed then add the vanilla extract and egg yolks and whisk again. Keep whisking while you weigh out the remaining ingredients.

4 Add the flour, baking powder, milk and lemon zest and fold in with a metal spoon. Spoon the mixture into the prepared tin, spread to level the top and bake in the preheated oven for about 20 minutes, or until a knife comes out clean.

5 While the cake is in the oven, make the meringue. Use a hand-held electric whisk to whisk the egg whites to stiff peaks, then add the sugar a little at a time, whisking well after each addition until the meringue is stiff and glossy.

6 Take the cake out of the oven, spread with the apple mixture and then pile the meringue on top. Return to the oven to bake for a further 15 minutes until the meringue is lightly golden.

PEAR FRANGIPANE CAKE

A delightful patisserie-style pudding. The combination of pear and almond frangipane is sublime. So quick and easy to put together, you really can make this at the last minute.

SERVES 8	MAKING TIME	BAKING TIME
	20 minutes	20–25 minutes

140 g unsalted butter

140 g caster sugar

3 large eggs

1 tsp vanilla extract

180 g ground almonds

60 g self-raising flour

4–5 pears, peeled, cored and sliced into six (hard pears are fine)

50 g flaked almonds

2 tbsp apricot jam, warmed

1 Preheat the oven to 180°C (350°F/Gas 4). Line a 20-cm tart tin (with fluted edge) or a shallow 20 x 30-cm tray bake tin with non-stick baking paper. I use a rectangular loosed-bottomed flan tin.

2 Cream together the butter and sugar, then beat in the eggs and vanilla extract. Fold in the ground almonds and self-raising flour.

3 Spoon the mixture into the prepared tin, arrange the thickly sliced pears on top and scatter with the flaked almonds.

4 Brush with the apricot jam and bake in the preheated oven for about 20 minutes, or until golden on top. This is best served warm but if you are not eating immediately, then leave to cool in the tin.

Miranda's variations

Finely chop 100 g of milk chocolate and sprinkle over the pears before baking.

Replace the pears with any fruit that is fresh and in season. Try 150g of raspberries with 2 teaspoons of grated lemon zest; 6 quartered plums with 2 teaspoons of grated orange zest; 6 quartered fresh figs with 2 teaspoons of grated orange zest – brush with honey instead of apricot jam.

BRAMLEY APPLE, RASPBERRY AND ALMOND BRITTLE CAKE

Crispy caramel almond brittle is the crowning glory on this delicious cake, packed full of apples and raspberries. Nothing further is required, except perhaps a dollop of clotted cream. A great cake to take to friends when you have offered to make pudding!

SERVES 6–8	MAKING TIME	BAKING TIME
	20 minutes	1 hour

225 g cooking apples, peeled, cored, and finely sliced

2 tbsp lemon juice

175 g unsalted butter, softened

150 g caster sugar

2 large eggs

1 tsp vanilla extract

225 g self-raising flour

50 g ground almonds

½ tsp salt

1 tsp baking powder

140 g crème fraîche

grated zest of 1 lemon

100–150 g fresh raspberries (do not wash)

For the topping

50 g unsalted butter

50 g demerara sugar

80 g flaked almonds

1 Preheat the oven to 180°C (350°F/Gas 4). Lightly oil a 23-cm round springform or loose-bottomed cake tin or deep flan dish and then dust with flour; alternatively, use a cake tin liner.

2 Put the chopped apples in a bowl with a squeeze of lemon juice to prevent discolouring and set aside.

3 Cream together the butter and sugar. Add the eggs and vanilla extract and beat well to combine. Then mix in the flour, ground almonds, salt, baking powder, crème fraîche and lemon zest.

4 Spoon half the mixture into the prepared tin and spread the apples evenly on top. Add the raspberries. Spoon the remaining cake mixture on top and level with a palette knife.

5 Stand the cake on a baking sheet (to prevent sticky drips) and then bake in the preheated oven.

6 Put all the topping ingredients in a pan, place over a low heat and, once the mixture starts to bubble, switch off the heat.

7 When the cake has been in the oven for 45 minutes remove from the oven (still on the baking sheet) and pour the almond topping over the top. Spread a little to ensure the whole top is covered then put the cake back into the oven to bake for a further 15 minutes. Allow to cool in the tin for about 10 minutes before serving while still warm.

SPECULOOS CAKE

Warm spices and aromatic cardamom enrich this dark chocolate and almond sour cream cake, which is sprinkled with toasted almonds and dusted with spiced cocoa powder.

SERVES 8	MAKING TIME	BAKING TIME
	20 minutes	45 minutes

200 g plain chocolate (I use Bournville)

225 g unsalted butter

4 large eggs

225 g dark brown sugar

1 tsp vanilla extract

100 g soured cream or natural yoghurt

175 g flaked almonds

175 ground almonds (or 100 g ground almonds and 75 g unskinned almonds, roughly chopped)

25 g cocoa powder

1 tsp baking powder

1 tbsp mixed spice

seeds from 6 cardamom pods, crushed

pinch of finely ground black pepper

pinch of salt

For the decoration

20 g toasted flaked almonds

2 tsp cocoa powder

½ tsp mixed spice

1 Preheat the oven to 170°C (325°F/Gas 3). Line a 20-cm cake tin with non-stick baking paper or use a cake tin liner as this mixture is very runny. If you don't have a tin liner then make sure you put the tin on a baking sheet to catch any spillages.

2 Melt the chocolate and butter in a bowl over a pan of simmering water. Put to one side to cool a little.

3 Whisk together the eggs, sugar and vanilla then whisk in the yoghurt or soured cream. Mix in all the remaining ingredients and stir well to combine.

4 Pour into the prepared tin (it will be very runny) and bake in the preheated oven for 45 minutes, or until a knife comes out clean.

5 Remove from the oven and leave to cool and firm up in the tin. Sprinkle with toasted flaked almonds and dust with the cocoa powder and mixed spice. Serve warm with crème fraîche.

ESPRESSO CAKE

Dark, intense and moody. This is delicious eaten while still warm, drizzled with cream, for a gluten-free chocolate-coffee fix.

SERVES 6

MAKING TIME
10 minutes

BAKING TIME
25 minutes

1 tbsp instant espresso powder, plus extra for dredging

115 g unsalted butter

175 g good-quality chocolate (70% cocoa solids)

150 g caster sugar

3 large eggs, beaten

60 g gluten-free cocoa powder, plus extra for dredging

¼ tsp salt

a few coffee beans, crushed, to decorate (optional)

1 Preheat the oven to 180°C (350°F/Gas 4) and line a 20-cm round cake tin with non-stick baking paper or a cake tin liner.

2 Mix the tablespoon of espresso powder with 1 teaspoon of boiling water. Place in a bowl with the butter and chocolate and set over a pan of simmering water. Add the sugar and stir until dissolved. Remove from the heat.

3 Use a balloon whisk to whisk in the eggs, then sift in the cocoa powder and salt and stir to combine. Scrape into the prepared tin and bake in the preheated oven for about 25 minutes or until dry on top and coming away from the sides of the tin.

4 Remove from the oven and leave in the tin to settle and cool a little. Dredge with cocoa and coffee powder or sprinkle with a few crushed coffee beans. Serve warm, cut into slices and drizzled with cream. Or, serve in thin slices with cups of coffee.

FLORENTINE CAKE

A thin layer of darkest 70% chocolate, hiding jewelled peel, glacé cherries and dried fruits baked in a brown sugar and almond cake. All the joys of a Florentine in a simple-to-make cake.

SERVES 6–8

MAKING TIME
15 minutes

BAKING TIME
20–25 minutes

150 g good-quality chocolate (70% cocoa solids)

75 g candied peel

100 g toasted flaked almonds

75 g raisins

75 g glacé cherries, halved

100g light muscovado sugar, plus 2 tbsp

100 g unsalted butter, softened

2 large eggs

100 g plain flour

1 tsp baking powder

50 g ground almonds

60 ml semi-skimmed milk

1 Preheat the oven to 180°C (350°F/Gas 4) and line the base of a 20-cm round cake tin with non-stick baking paper.

2 Break the chocolate into the base of the cake tin and pop into the oven as it is warming up – it should take about 5 minutes to melt.

3 Remove the tin from the oven and spread the chocolate out with a knife to cover the base. Sprinkle the candied peel, almonds, raisins and cherries over the chocolate and then top with 2 tablespoons of the sugar.

4 Mix together all the remaining ingredients except the milk, either by hand or in an electric mixer. Add the milk once everything has been mixed together.

5 Spread on top of the dried fruit and chocolate and smooth to level the surface. Bake in the preheated oven for about 20–25 minutes or until a skewer comes out clean.

6 Leave to cool completely in the tin then turn out on to a plate and carefully remove the baking paper from the chocolate layer. The bottom of the cake will now be the top!

PLUMBLE CAKE

Plums, toasted hazelnuts and brown sugar crumble come together in one cake – the delicious plum juices seep into the roasted hazelnut crumble on top. This was christened 'plumble cake' by my children, who could never say plum crumble cake when they were little!

SERVES 6–8	MAKING TIME	BAKING TIME
	20 minutes	40–45 minutes

200 g self-raising flour

175 g light muscovado sugar

1 tsp baking powder

150 g ground almonds

3 large eggs, lightly beaten

50 ml semi-skimmed milk

100 ml natural yoghurt

1 tsp vanilla extract

175 g unsalted butter, softened

6 plums, stoned and halved

For the crumble

50 g unsalted butter

100 g plain flour

50 g demerara sugar

50 g chopped roasted hazelnuts

1 Preheat the oven to 180°C (350°F/Gas 4) and line a 23-cm loose-bottomed round tin with non-stick baking paper or use a 20 x 30-cm tray bake tin – a deep patisserie tin is ideal.

2 Sift the flour, sugar, baking powder and ground almonds into a bowl and stir to combine, or whizz together in a food processor.

3 In a jug, mix together the eggs, milk, yoghurt and vanilla extract with a fork. Add to the dry ingredients along with the softened butter and mix well to combine, either by hand or in the food processor.

4 Pour into the prepared tin and arrange the plums on top, flat side up. Bake in the preheated oven for 20 minutes.

5 While the cake is in the oven, make the crumble. Rub the butter into the flour (this is super quick in a food processor but you can use your fingertips), then stir or whizz in the sugar and nuts.

6 Remove the cake from the oven after 20 minutes, sprinkle with the crumble mixture and then return to the oven for a further 20–25 minutes, until the top is golden and crunchy and the cake is coming away from the sides of the tin. This is best eaten straight from the oven.

Miranda's variation

This is also delicious made with rhubarb, blackberries or fresh figs instead of the plums.

DOUBLE CHOCOLATE BROWNIE MERINGUE CAKE

Here the lightest chocolate brownie studded with melting pieces of plain chocolate sits beneath a generous layer of tempting chocolate meringue.

SERVES 6–8	MAKING TIME	BAKING TIME
	20 minutes	35 minutes

220 g good-quality chocolate (70% cocoa solids)

200 g unsalted butter

250 g icing sugar

3 large eggs

110 g plain flour

For the chocolate meringue

3 large egg whites

½ tsp cream of tartar

150 g caster sugar

2 tbsp cocoa powder, sifted

Miranda's variation

Make the brownie base as above but press 100 g of fresh raspberries into the brownie mixture before baking. Make the meringue topping as above but fold in 50 g of chopped roasted hazelnuts before heaping on top of the cake. Scatter with a further 50 g of hazelnuts and bake as above.

1 Preheat the oven to 190°C (375°F/Gas 5) and line a 23-cm round loose-bottomed cake tin with non-stick baking paper – a shallow sandwich tin is best.

2 Melt 180 g of the chocolate in a bowl over a pan of simmering water and set aside. Chop the remaining chocolate and keep for later.

3 Cream the butter and icing sugar in an electric mixer fitted with a paddle attachment until light, creamy and fluffy. Add the eggs one at a time, whisking well after each one. Gradually add the flour and beat well until very smooth.

4 Slowly pour in the melted chocolate, mix thoroughly, then add the chopped chocolate at the last minute. Pour into the prepared tin and bake in the preheated oven for 10 minutes.

5 While the cake is in the oven, make the meringue topping. Whisk the egg whites and cream of tartar until stiff peaks form then slowly whisk in the caster sugar in roughly four amounts, whisking after each addition. Add the sifted cocoa powder with the last addition.

6 When the brownie has been in the oven for 10 minutes, reduce the temperature to 170°C (325°F/Gas 3). Remove from the oven, spread the meringue carefully on top of the part-baked brownie and return to the oven for a further 25 minutes until the meringue is firm on top.

FIG, CARAMEL AND MASCARPONE CAKE

Fresh figs and caramel are baked into the lightest buttery vanilla cake. Sandwiched with a creamy mascarpone icing and drizzled with caramel, this is a piece of heaven on a plate.

SERVES 8	MAKING TIME	BAKING TIME
	25 minutes	20–25 minutes

225 g unsalted butter, softened

225 g caster sugar

4 large eggs

1 tsp vanilla extract

225 g self-raising flour

2 tsp baking powder

6 ripe figs, chopped, plus 1 or 2 extra to decorate

150 g dulce de leche (I use Nestlé Carnation Caramel)

For the filling

175 g mascarpone

175 g icing sugar, plus extra to decorate

1 tsp vanilla extract

150 g dulce de leche (I use Nestlé Carnation Caramel)

1 Preheat the oven to 180°C (350°F/Gas 4) and line two 20-cm round loose-bottomed cake tins with non-stick baking paper.

2 Put all the ingredients except the figs and caramel into a large bowl or mixer and mix well until well combined.

3 Put half of the chopped figs into the base of each tin and spoon the mixture equally between the two tins, on top of the figs. Dollop the caramel on top of each one and use a palette knife or spoon to swirl the caramel into the cake mixture. Smooth the top of the mixture and then bake in the preheated oven for 20–25 minutes or until a skewer comes out clean.

4 Beat together the mascarpone, icing sugar and vanilla extract for the filling using a food processor, hand-held mixer or large bowl and wooden spoon.

5 Remove the cakes from the oven and leave to cool in their tins for at least 10 minutes before turning them out on to wire racks.

6 When the cakes are cool, spread one cake with a layer of mascarpone icing, then spread a layer of caramel on top. Put the other cake on top.

7 Chop the remaining fig into slices and place on top of the cake. Drizzle with any remaining caramel sauce and dust with icing sugar, if you like. This is best eaten immediately or the same day.

STRAWBERRY MACARON CAKE

Delightful almond macarons are layered with strawberries and vanilla-scented mascarpone cream to make this pretty yet sophisticated cake. Quicker to make and bake than you could imagine, this is a cake with which to impress.

SERVES 8–10	MAKING TIME	BAKING TIME
	40 minutes	20 minutes

250 g ground almonds

350 g icing sugar

6 large egg whites

pinch of salt

150 g caster sugar

50 g toasted flaked almonds, to decorate

icing sugar, to decorate

For the filling

300 ml double cream

250 g mascarpone

1 tsp vanilla extract

1 tbsp caster sugar

6 tbsp good-quality strawberry jam

200 g fresh strawberries, roughly quartered

fresh redcurrants, to decorate

1 Preheat the oven to 160°C (325°F/Gas 3) and line three baking sheets with non-stick baking paper. Draw a 23-cm circle in pencil on each one (use a cake tin as a guide).

2 Put the ground almonds and icing sugar into a bowl and stir to combine. In a separate bowl, whisk the egg whites with a pinch of salt to soft peaks then whisk in the caster sugar, a little at a time, until the mixture is thick and glossy.

3 Use a large metal spoon to fold the icing sugar and ground almonds into the glossy egg whites.

4 Spoon three circles of the mixture on to the prepared baking sheets and use a palette knife to level off. Give the baking sheets a sharp tap on the worktop to ensure a good base on the macaron (also known as a 'foot'). Leave them to stand at room temperature for about 15 minutes to form a slight skin on the surface of the macarons.

4 Put the macarons into the preheated oven to bake for about 20 minutes until crisp around the edges. Remove from the oven and leave to cool on the paper on the baking sheets.

5 Make the filling. Whisk together the cream, mascarpone, vanilla extract and sugar until stiff peaks form. Put in a covered bowl in the fridge until you are ready to assemble and serve the cake.

Recipe continues overleaf

6 Carefully remove each macaron from the baking paper. Place the first one on your serving plate and spread with 3 tablespoons of jam. Slather on about one-third of the mascarpone cream and scatter over about one-third of the chopped strawberries. Place another macaron on top and repeat the jam, mascarpone and strawberry layers. Place the last macaron on the top of your cake. Spread the remaining mascarpone cream on top and decorate with strawberries and the redcurrants, if using. Sprinkle with toasted flaked almonds and dust with icing sugar to finish.

....

NOTES

I often take a pudding cake like this round to a friend's house when asked to bring a pudding for supper. I take it as a 'kit' packed in a basket and assemble it when you arrive. You will need:

Stacked macaroon cakes still on their baking paper on the baking sheet – wrap in foil to transport: mascarpone cream whipped and transported in a covered bowl; strawberries, jam and toasted almonds in small containers; icing sugar in a shaker; serving plate.

....

PISTACHIO AND DARK CHOCOLATE MACARON CAKE

Two large pistachio-green macarons are layered with rich chocolate ganache. This is the kind of cake at which I gaze longingly in the windows of French patisseries. Easy to make and surprisingly quick to bake.

SERVES 8	MAKING TIME	BAKING TIME
	30 minutes	30 minutes

6 large egg whites

pinch of salt

150 g granulated sugar

225 g pistachio nuts

125 g ground almonds

350 g icing sugar

cocoa powder, for dusting

For the ganache

200 g plain chocolate (I use Bournville), roughly chopped

200 ml double cream

1 Preheat the oven to 170°C (325°F/Gas 3) and line two baking sheets with non-stick baking paper. Use a pencil to draw two 20-cm circles on the reverse of the baking paper – I draw round the base of a cake tin.

2 Make the ganache by placing the chopped chocolate and cream in a bowl over a pan of simmering water. Once the chocolate has melted, remove the bowl from the heat and stir well to combine. Leave to cool at room temperature or pop in the fridge if you are in a mad rush!

3 Whisk the egg whites with a pinch of salt until stiff peaks form. Add one-third of the granulated sugar and then whisk on high speed for 1 minute. Repeat until all the granulated sugar has been incorporated.

4 Whizz 125 g of the pistachio nuts in a food processor with the ground almonds and icing sugar, until finely chopped. Fold into the egg-white mixture using a large metal spoon.

5 Spoon half the mixture on to each prepared baking sheet and use a palette knife to spread into circles and smooth the top. Give each baking sheet a sharp tap on the worktop – this helps to give the macarons a good base. Leave to stand on the worktop uncovered for about 20 minutes.

6 Bake in the preheated oven for about 30 minutes, until crisp around the edges. Leave to cool on the baking sheets until completely cold. I have broken many with my impatience!

7 Just before serving, sandwich together with the ganache. Roughly chop the remaining pistachio nuts, scatter over the top and then dust with cocoa powder.

HAZELNUT TIRAMISU CAKE

Roasted hazelnut cakes are drizzled with hot coffee and Marsala, and layered with mascarpone cream. Pour the warm chocolate over the top and let it drip temptingly down the side.

SERVES 8	MAKING TIME	BAKING TIME
	30 minutes	30 minutes

200 g hazelnuts

225 g unsalted butter

225 g caster sugar

1 tsp vanilla extract

2 tsp grated orange zest

4 large eggs plus 2 yolks

200 g self-raising flour

120 ml semi-skimmed milk

For the mascarpone cream

185 ml double cream

250 g mascarpone

100 g icing sugar

1 tbsp Marsala

For the chocolate topping

150 g good-quality chocolate
   (70% cocoa solids)

25 g unsalted butter

½ tsp sea salt

For the coffee soak

1 tbsp instant coffee powder

2 tsp caster sugar

1 tbsp Marsala

grated plain chocolate, toasted
   hazelnuts or crushed
   coffee beans, to decorate

1 Preheat the oven to 180°C (350°F/Gas 4) and line two 20-cm round loose-bottomed cake tins with non-stick baking paper or use cake tin liners.

2 Put the hazelnuts on a baking sheet and place in the oven as it preheats to toast them for about 8 minutes. Leave to cool for about 10 minutes, then roughly chop about a quarter of the nuts and set aside. Whizz the remaining nuts in a food processor until finely chopped.

3 Put the butter, sugar, vanilla extract and orange zest in the bowl of an electric mixer and whisk together at a high speed for about 3 minutes until pale and fluffy.

4 Add the eggs and egg yolks and whisk again to combine. Fold in the flour and ground hazelnuts and once this is combined, fold in the chopped hazelnuts and milk. Spoon into the prepared tins and bake in the preheated oven for about 30 minutes until springy to the touch.

5 While the cakes are baking, make the mascarpone cream. Whisk the cream then fold in the mascarpone, icing sugar and Marsala. Set aside.

6 Melt the chocolate for the topping in a bowl over a pan of simmering water and, once melted, stir in the butter and salt.

7 Mix the coffee, sugar and Marsala with 2 tablespoons of boiling water and pour over the cakes as soon as they come out of the oven. Allow to cool in the tin for 10 minutes before turning out, or leave to cool completely in the tin if you prefer.

8 Just before serving, sandwich the cakes together with mascarpone cream, put another thick layer of the mascarpone cream on the top and then drizzle with the chocolate topping. Decorate with grated plain chocolate or sprinkle with a toasted hazelnuts and crushed coffee beans.

CARAMEL CREAM CHEESECAKE WITH SALTED TOFFEE PECANS

Rich golden caramel cake baked with swirls of creamy vanilla cheesecake. This indulgent pudding is packed with morsels of delicious crunchy salted toffee pecans and chunks of meltingly good fudge. Just when you thought cakes couldn't get any better…

SERVES 6–8	MAKING TIME 20 minutes	BAKING TIME 35 minutes

100 g pecan nuts

100 g chopped fudge

1 tsp sea salt

100 g unsalted butter

100 g white chocolate

100 g soft light brown sugar

90 ml water

2 tsp golden syrup

2 tsp vanilla extract

2 large eggs (1 for the cheesecake and 1 for the cream-cheese swirl)

130 g plain flour

2 tsp baking powder

140 g full-fat cream cheese

65 g caster sugar

1 Preheat the oven to 180°C (350°F/Gas 4) and line a deep 20-cm springform cake tin with non-stick baking paper or use a cake tin liner.

2 Sprinkle 70 g of the pecans, half the fudge and the sea salt over the base of the lined tin and pop in the oven while it is preheating (about 10 minutes).

3 Heat the butter, white chocolate, brown sugar, water, syrup and 1 teaspoon of vanilla extract in a bowl over a pan of simmering water (or in the microwave in short bursts, stirring in between to check the chocolate doesn't burn). Once the mixture has melted, whisk together with a balloon whisk to combine.

4 Add 1 egg, whisk again, then whisk in the flour and baking powder.

5 In a small bowl, beat together the cream cheese, the remaining egg, the caster sugar and remaining vanilla extract with a wooden spoon – don't worry of the mixture isn't completely smooth.

6 Take the cake tin out of the oven, spoon the cake mixture into it and then dollop on the cream cheese mixture. Sprinkle with the remaining nuts and fudge and bake in the preheated oven for 30–35 minutes until golden and almost firm. Leave to cool in the tin.

TARTE AU CITRON CAKE

A French classic translated into cake form. A delicate golden layer of madeleine sponge has a traditional lemon custard baked on top.

SERVES 6	MAKING TIME	BAKING TIME
	20 minutes	40 minutes

4 large eggs

100 g caster sugar

80 g unsalted butter, melted

1 tsp vanilla extract

100 g plain flour

40 g ground almonds

pinch of salt

1 tsp baking powder

icing sugar, for dredging

For the lemon custard

6 large eggs

150 ml cream

270 g caster sugar

grated zest and juice of 3 lemons

1 Preheat the oven to 180°C (350°F/Gas 4). Line a deep 20-cm springform cake tin with non-stick baking paper or, ideally, use a paper cake tin liner. Alternatively use a loose-bottomed deep flan tin.

2 Using either a mixer or an electric hand-held whisk, whisk the eggs at high speed for about 5 minutes. Add the sugar a little at a time, while continuing to whisk at high speed.

3 Gently fold in the melted butter and vanilla extract, then fold in the flour, ground almonds, salt and baking powder.

4 Scrape the mixture into the prepared tin and level with a palette knife. Stand the tin on a baking sheet and bake in the preheated oven for about 15 minutes until pale golden and springy to the touch.

5 While the cake is in the oven, make the lemon custard. Put the eggs into a large jug and whisk with a balloon whisk. Add the rest of the custard ingredients and whisk well to combine.

6 Take the cake out of the oven and quickly pour the custard on top. Return to the oven to bake for a further 20 minutes or until the topping looks set and is firm to the touch.

7 Remove from the oven and leave to cool in the tin for at least half an hour, or chill in the fridge and remove half an hour before serving. Carefully take out of the tin, remove the baking paper or cake liner and dredge with icing sugar before serving.

PARTY CAKES

MERINGUES WITH RASPBERRY CREAM

Crisp on the outside and marshmallowy in the middle, the pale meringue contrasts perfectly with the pink raspberry cream to make a pretty teatime or pudding treat. This recipe can be used to make three different meringue confections: a stunning meringue cake sandwiched and topped with layers of raspberry cream and crowned with slender white candles; tiny meringue kisses delicately partnered with pink raspberry cream; or luscious large meringue swirls baked with fresh raspberries inside.

MAKES 1 MERINGUE CAKE, ABOUT 20 MERINGUE KISSES, OR 12 LARGE RASPBERRY SWIRLS	MAKING TIME 15–20 minutes	BAKING TIME 1–3 hours

4 large egg whites

170 g caster sugar

170 g granulated sugar

For the raspberry cream

200 ml double cream

100 g icing sugar

50 g raspberries, squashed with a fork

For the raspberry meringue swirls

150 g raspberries, squashed with a fork (leave a few whole)

1 Preheat the oven to 120°C (250°F/Gas ½). Line two baking sheets with non-stick baking paper.

2 Whisk the egg whites in a clean bowl until stiff peaks form. With the machine running on high speed, add the caster sugar, a tablespoon at a time. Whisk until stiff and glossy.

3 Reduce the speed and sprinkle in the granulated sugar, a tablespoon at a time. Whisk well after each addition and continue until the meringue is glossy and well combined.

4 To make the raspberry cream, whisk the cream until stiff, then use a metal spoon to fold in the icing sugar and squashed raspberries. Chill in the fridge until ready to fill the meringues.

5 To make the **meringue cake**, draw a 20cm circle on each piece of baking paper (use a cake tin as a guide). Divide the meringue mixture between the two baking sheets and use a palette knife to create two meringue discs. Bake in the preheated oven for about 1 hour, then reduce the temperature to 100°C (200°F/Gas ¼) and bake for a further 2 hours – alternatively you can switch the oven off and leave the meringue inside with the door closed overnight. The meringue is baked when it comes cleanly away from the baking paper. When the meringue is completely cool, sandwich together with raspberry cream and spread more on the top.

6 To make the **meringue kisses**, transfer the meringue to a piping bag. Pipe about 40 meringues – each one should be 2 cm across – on to the prepared baking sheets. Bake in the preheated oven for 45 minutes–1 hour or bake for 45 minutes, turn off the oven and leave the meringues inside for a further hour (or overnight), which will make them more marshmallowy. Just before serving, sandwich the meringues together with the raspberry cream. Enjoy immediately.

7 To make the **raspberry swirl meringues**, fold the 150 g of squashed raspberries into the meringue mixture. Use a large spoon to dollop generous heaps of the meringue on to the prepared baking sheets. Bake in the preheated oven for 1 hour then reduce the temperature to 100°C (200°/Gas ¼) and bake for a further 2 hours (check after 1½ hours). If they sound hollow and come cleanly away from the baking paper they are ready.

Miranda's variations

To make lemony meringues, sandwich the meringues together with a lemon cream: simply stir 110 g full-fat Greek yoghurt, about 6–8 tablespoons lemon curd and 2 teaspoons grated lemon zest into 200 ml whipped double cream. This is also delicious with the pulp and seeds of 2 passion fruit stirred into the lemon curd cream. Decorate the top of a lemon cream-filled meringue cake with finely grated lemon zest (or crystallised lemon zest). You could also make swirled lemon meringues – simply swirl 2 teaspoons of lemon curd and 2 teaspoons lemon zest into the meringue mixture before baking.

THREE-TIERED LEMON BLOSSOM CAKE

A delicious three-tiered zesty lemon cake, sandwiched with a lemon curd buttercream and topped with fresh white icing and pretty blossom decorations or crystallised edible flowers.

SERVES AT LEAST 8	MAKING TIME	BAKING TIME
	30 minutes, plus decorating	25 minutes

300 g unsalted butter, softened

300 g caster sugar

6 large eggs, lightly beaten

250 g self-raising flour

50 g cornflour

1½ tsp baking powder

grated zest of 2 lemons

juice of 1 lemon

For the buttercream

110 g unsalted butter, softened

400 g icing sugar

6 tbsp fresh lemon juice

3 tbsp lemon curd

1 tbsp grated lemon zest

For the icing

500 g royal icing sugar

6 tbsp fresh lemon juice

sugar flowers, to decorate

1 Preheat the oven to 180°C (350°F/Gas 4) and line three 20-cm round sandwich cake tins with non-stick baking paper. If you have only two tins, bake two cakes first and then reuse one of the tins to bake the third cake.

2 Put the softened butter and caster sugar into the bowl of an electric mixer and whisk until creamy and fluffy. Add the eggs, roughly one at a time, and whisk in well after each addition.

3 Sift the flour, cornflour and baking powder into a bowl and add to the egg mix a little at a time – fold in gently with a large metal spoon. Fold in the lemon zest with the last bit of flour.

4 Once all the flour is completely combined, gently fold in the lemon juice a little at a time.

5 Spoon a third of the mixture into each cake tin and gently level the tops with a palette knife. Bake in the preheated oven for about 20 minutes, or until springy to the touch and pale golden on top. Remove the cakes from the oven and leave them to cool in their tins before carefully turning them on to a wire rack.

6 Make the buttercream. Put the butter, half the icing sugar and the lemon juice in a large bowl and use an electric hand-held whisk to beat for about 3 minutes. Add the remaining icing sugar, the lemon curd and lemon zest and beat again for a further 2–3 minutes, until smooth, light and creamy.

7 Make the icing. Beat together the royal icing sugar and lemon juice for about 10 minutes in an electric mixer – you may need to add a little more lemon juice if the icing is too stiff.

8 Once the cakes are completely cold, sandwich together with the buttercream. Use a palette knife to carefully spread the icing on top of the cake – the icing should be at least 5 mm thick. Dip the palette knife in a little hot water to achieve a smooth finish. Leave the icing to firm up a little before decorating with sugar flowers or crystallised edible flowers (see page 9 for instructions).

Miranda's variation

For an even speedier version, this cake also looks and tastes stunning topped with the lemon curd buttercream instead of the icing. Tie a wide pastel-coloured ribbon around the outside for a pretty finish.

HEAVENLY CHOCOLATE CAKE

I make this cake for everyone's birthdays and it always goes down a storm. Dark chocolate sponge cake, enriched with melted chocolate to deepen the flavour, is slathered with thick, exceedingly chocolatey buttercream. Decorated with delicate sugar flowers, this is the prettiest, yet simplest cake to make. This makes one 20-cm, 3-tiered round cake or one 20-cm, 2-tiered cake and 12 cupcakes.

SERVES AT LEAST 8	MAKING TIME	BAKING TIME
	30 minutes	20–25 minutes

300 g unsalted butter, softened

300 g caster sugar

90 g good-quality chocolate (70% cocoa solids), melted

6 large eggs, lightly beaten

225 g self-raising flour

75 g cocoa powder

1½ tsp baking powder

For the chocolate buttercream

225 g unsalted butter, softened

450 g icing sugar, sifted

1½ tsp vanilla extract

4½ tbsp semi-skimmed milk

265 g good-quality chocolate (70% cocoa solids)

sugar flowers, to decorate

1 Preheat the oven to 180°C (350°F/Gas 4) and line three 18-cm round sandwich cake tins. If you have only two tins you can bake two cakes first, remove from their tins to cool on a wire rack and use one of the tins again to bake the third cake.

2 Cream together the butter and caster sugar in an electric mixer until light and fluffy. Add the melted chocolate and mix again.

3 Add the eggs a little at a time, beating well after each addition and checking they are fully incorporated before adding more to the mixture.

4 Sift the flour, cocoa powder and baking powder into a large bowl. With a metal spoon or large palette knife, fold the dry ingredients into the cake mixture, adding a little at a time.

5 Divide the mixture equally between the three prepared tins. Bake the cakes in the preheated oven for 20–25 minutes, or until springy to the touch. Leave the cakes to settle in their tins for about 10 minutes before carefully removing them from their tins and putting them to cool on a wire rack.

6 If the cakes are not completely level you may wish to trim the tops a little so the three tiers stack neatly – wait until they have completely cooled before doing this.

7 Make the buttercream. Put the butter in a mixing bowl with the icing sugar, vanilla extract and milk. Beat very firmly – ideally with a hand-held mixer or in a food processor. After about 2–3 minutes, the mixture should be smooth, creamy and quite fluffy.

8 Melt the chocolate over a pan of simmering water or very carefully in the microwave (do this in 20-second bursts and stir before heating again). Add the chocolate to the buttercream and beat again – it will thicken the more you beat it!

9 Once the cakes are completely cold, sandwich together with generous layers of chocolate buttercream and spread thickly on top.

10 Decorate the top with a selection of pretty sugar flower decorations and a few scattered around the sides of the cake in the buttercream layers.

Miranda's variations

For a summer berry cake, omit the sugar decorations and pile with fresh summer berries, putting lots around the base of the cake too.

For an even more indulgent party cake, make a double quantity of the ganache on page 26, sandwich the cake together with buttercream and then spread ganache over the top and sides. Decorate with berries, fresh flowers, chocolate truffles or sugar decorations. Perfect for evening parties or as a sumptuous pudding.

Turn into a fantastic children's party cake by decorating with smarties, flake bars, chocolate buttons and cake sparklers. Replace the 70 per cent cocoa chocolate with a sweeter dark chocolate, such as Bournville.

The recipe above will make 36 delicious cupcakes. Decorate with swirls of chocolate buttercream and pretty decorations or, for a wedding or christening, decorate with white chocolate buttercream (see page 64) and decorate.

For a chocolate Easter cake, decorate with mini eggs and fluffy chicks or delicate crystallised flowers (see page 9 for instructions).

PURE AND SIMPLE CAKE

This four-tiered, buttery vanilla cake is simply frosted with pale buttercream. Tall, simple and elegant.

SERVES AT LEAST 8	MAKING TIME	BAKING TIME
	30 minutes	45 minutes, plus
		30 minutes to ice and decorate

500 g unsalted butter, softened

450 g caster sugar

2 vanilla pods, slit lengthways and seeds removed, or 2 tsp vanilla extract

6 large eggs

480 g self-raising flour

300 ml semi-skimmed milk

For the buttercream

225 g unsalted butter, softened

500 g icing sugar, sifted

2 tsp vanilla extract

pinch of salt

2–3 tbsp milk or double cream

DECORATING IDEAS

- Cut triangles of pretty fabric and use to make miniature bunting to thread between two wooden skewers. Decorate with edible flowers such as pansies and primroses.

- For a simple wintry decoration, tie a bunch of rosemary with a velvet ribbon and lie it on top of the cake. Press fresh cranberries around the base of the cake.

1 Preheat the oven to 180°C (350°F/Gas 4) and line two 20-cm round cake tins with non-stick baking paper.

2 Cream together the butter, sugar and the seeds from the vanilla pods in an electric mixer, then beat in the eggs. Whisk at high speed to incorporate lots of air.

3 Fold in the flour and then the milk. Spoon into the prepared tins and smooth to level the tops. Bake in the preheated oven for 45 minutes, or until springy to the touch.

4 Remove from the oven and leave to cool in their tins for at least 10 minutes before carefully turning out on to a wire rack. When the cakes are completely cold, slice each cake in half horizontally so you have four slim round cakes. Trim the tops level if any are domed.

5 Make the buttercream. Put the softened butter into a mixer and use the paddle attachment to beat the butter on a medium speed for 3–4 minutes – this will make it paler in colour. Add the icing sugar, a quarter at a time, mixing on high speed for about 30 seconds before adding more. Add the vanilla and salt and mix at a high speed to combine. Finally, add the milk or cream a tablespoon at a time. If you add too much, add an additional tablespoon of icing sugar and beat again. Mix until you have a creamy, smooth and pale buttercream.

6 Put the first cake on to a flat plate or cake stand, add a layer of buttercream and repeat until you have used all four cakes. Use a palette knife to cover the sides and top of the cake with the remaining buttercream. This should look hand finished and rustic so don't worry about making it perfectly smooth.

MUCH-LOVED FAMILY FRUIT CAKE

This cake has been made for weddings, christenings and every Christmas for at least three generations of my family. I hope it will find a special place in creating memories for you and your loved ones.

MAKES ONE 23-CM CAKE	MAKING TIME	BAKING TIME
	30 minutes, plus decorating	3 hours

225 g currants

200 g glacé cherries

175 g sultanas

115 g dried cranberries

225 g dried apricots, chopped

115 g blanched whole almonds, roughly chopped (optional)

175 ml brandy

250 g unsalted butter, softened

100 g soft brown sugar

150 g caster sugar

6 large eggs, lightly beaten

225 g plain flour

225 g ground almonds

1 tbsp cocoa powder

½ tsp ground nutmeg

½ tsp mixed spice

½ tsp salt

grated zest of 1 orange

grated zest of 1 lemon

1 tsp vanilla extract

To ice the cake

1 x 340-g jar apricot jam

icing sugar, for dusting

500 g marzipan

500 g ready-to-roll white icing

23-cm cake board (or slightly larger if you prefer)

1 Put all the dried fruit and the almonds (if using) in a large bowl. Pour over the brandy, and stir to coat the fruit. Cover the bowl, and leave the fruit to steep until you are ready to use it. (If you are super organised then steep overnight before baking the cake.)

2 Preheat the oven to 150°C (300°F/Gas 2) and line the base and sides of a deep 23-cm round cake tin with a double layer of non-stick baking paper.

3 Put the butter and the two sugars in the bowl of an electric mixer and mix until light and fluffy (this usually takes about 5 minutes on medium speed). Add the eggs a little at a time with the mixer still running; mix until well incorporated.

4 Add all of the remaining ingredients and the brandy-soaked fruits and mix on a low speed until well combined.

5 Spoon the mixture into the prepared tin and smooth the top gently. Cut a double layer circle of non-stick baking paper the same size as the top of the cake and cut a hole in the middle. Place on top of the cake. Place a wide strip of brown paper around the outside of the cake tin and tie with string.

6 Put the cake on the bottom shelf of the preheated oven and bake for about 3 hours. Check whether the cake is done by inserting a skewer into the centre; it should come out clean. If the skewer is sticky, return to the oven for a further 15 minutes. Allow to cool in the tin for at least 30 minutes, then turn out on to a wire rack and remove the baking paper.

Recipe continues overleaf

7 When the cake is completely cool, you are ready to ice. Warm the apricot jam in a pan, and then pass it through a sieve. Level the top of the cake by cutting the top off with a serrated knife, brush the levelled top with a little apricot jam, then place it upside down on top of the cake board. Use a piece of string to measure the top and sides of the fruit cake (this is so that you roll the marzipan out to the right size). Paint the fruit cake all over with the apricot jam.

8 Dust your work surface with icing sugar and roll the marzipan out until it is large enough to cover the top and sides of the fruit cake. Carefully lift the marzipan on to the cake and smooth it on with your hands. Trim off any excess marzipan, ensuring the cake board is also covered. Repeat with the ready-to-roll icing.

DECORATING IDEAS

- Christening cake: tie a wide ribbon around the cake (pale blue or pink gingham, or plain) and make a bow – for a 23-cm cake you will need at least 160cm. Stick tiny pale blue or pink sugar paste blossom flowers on to the top of the cake in the shape of the child's name. To do this, draw around the cake tin on a piece of white paper and then write the name in the middle of the circle. Lay the paper on the cake and use a pin to prick the outline of the name through the paper. Remove the paper and, using the pricked lines as a guide, stick on the sugar paste flowers with icing.

- Christmas cake: ice the cake as above and then tie a wide, Christmassy ribbon around the outside. Roll out the icing offcuts and use a Christmas-shaped biscuit cutter to cut out shapes. Stick them to the top of the cake with a few dabs of water.

- Spring wedding cake: decorate the iced cake with sugar paste flowers or crystallised fresh primroses. Tie a wide white ribbon around the cake.

- Rose and daisy cake: sit the iced cake on a cake dummy that is 2.5 cm smaller than the cake itself. Push roses and Michaelmas daisies into the dummy to create a pretty base for the cake. Tie a small bunch of roses with a thin piece of ribbon and place on top of the iced cake. Finally tie a wide pink organza ribbon around the cake and tie in a loose bow.

DAISY CHAIN ANGEL CAKES

The lightest, palest lemon-scented angel cake is baked in a tray bake tin and simply sliced into petit four sized squares. Covered with mascarpone cream and decorated with sugar daisies, these delightful little cakes sit prettily on a tea party table.

MAKES AT LEAST 20	MAKING TIME	BAKING TIME
	30 minutes	35–40 minutes

8 large egg whites

¼ tsp salt

1 tsp cream of tartar

grated zest of 1 lemon

50 g caster sugar

200 g icing sugar

140 g plain flour

For the icing

175 ml double cream

225 g mascarpone

250 g icing sugar

4 tbsp lemon curd

2 tsp grated lemon zest

sugar daisy decorations,
   to decorate

1 Preheat the oven to 180° (350°F/Gas 4) and line a 20 x 30-cm tray bake tin with non-stick baking paper.

2 Put the egg whites into the bowl of an electric mixer and whisk for about 1 minute at high speed. Add the salt, cream of tartar and lemon zest and whisk again until soft peaks form.

3 Add a couple of tablespoons of caster sugar, whisk at high speed then add a couple of tablespoons of icing sugar and whisk again. Continue in this way until all the caster sugar and icing sugar has been incorporated.

4 Sift the flour into the bowl and gently fold into the egg-white mixture with a metal spoon.

5 Scrape the mixture into the prepared tin and gently level the top with a palette knife.

6 Bake in the preheated oven for 30–35 minutes until springy to the touch. Leave to cool in the tin and when completely cold, remove from the tin and cut into 3-cm squares. Slice each in half and cut off the edges.

7 Make the icing. Whip the cream until stiff then mix in the mascarpone, icing sugar, lemon curd and lemon zest. Use a palette knife to cover the top and sides of each cake. Decorate with some sugar daisies.

LAVENDER MADELEINES

Madeleines are dainty, traditional French sponge cakes that have a distinctive shell-like shape, which come from their being baked in madeleine tins. These elegant, lavender-infused cakes are perfect for tea parties and are best enjoyed while still slightly warm.

MAKES ABOUT 24	MAKING TIME	BAKING TIME
	15 minutes	12 minutes

80 g unsalted butter

2 tbsp lavender flowers, stalks removed

4 large eggs

100 g caster sugar

1 tsp vanilla extract

140 g plain flour (or 100 g plain flour and 40 g ground almonds)

1 tsp grated lemon zest

½ tsp baking powder

pinch of salt

icing sugar, to dust

1 Preheat the oven to 180° (350°F/Gas 4) and oil and flour two 12-hole madeleine tins. I find this easiest to do with spray oil.

2 Put the butter and lavender in a small bowl and melt in the microwave or in a small pan over a low heat. Stir to combine and leave to stand.

3 Whisk the eggs at high speed in an electric mixer or using an electric hand-held whisk for about 5 minutes. Add the sugar a little at a time, while continuing to whisk at high speed.

4 Strain the butter using a fine sieve to remove the lavender flowers, and gently fold the melted butter and vanilla extract into the egg-and-sugar mixture. Then fold in the flour (or flour and almonds), lemon zest, baking powder and salt.

5 Spoon the mixture into the prepared madeleine tins (take care not to overfill – about 1 tablespoon of batter per madeleine is about right) and bake in the preheated oven for about 8–12 minutes or until golden. This will vary depending on the size of your madeleine tins.

6 Remove the madeleines from the oven, lay a clean tea towel over the top of the cakes and turn over so that the tea towel is on the work surface and the tin upside down. Gently tap the tin and the madeleines should fall out. Otherwise use a palette knife to gently ease them from their shells. Carefully lift the madeleines on to a cooling rack. Dust with icing sugar before serving.

MIDSUMMER STRAWBERRY CAKE

I love the Scandinavian tradition of celebrating Midsummer with strawberry cake. I enjoy making this on hot balmy days when strawberries are bountiful and the evenings are long. It is a wonderful centerpiece for meals in the garden or for a summery tea party and always makes me feel poetic, as if I were making it for Titania in *A Midsummer Night's Dream*…

SERVES AT LEAST 8	MAKING TIME	BAKING TIME
	30 minutes	20–25 minutes

340 g unsalted butter, softened

340 g caster sugar

1 vanilla pod, slit lengthways and seeds removed, or 1 tsp vanilla extract

6 large eggs, lightly beaten

340 g self-raising flour

1 tsp baking powder

1 tbsp semi-skimmed milk

For the filling

340 g unsalted butter

1 tsp vanilla extract

600 g icing sugar

500 g fresh strawberries (unwashed)

For the icing (optional)

300 g icing sugar

5–6 tsp strawberry purée (see step 6)

To decorate

edible flowers

rose petals

strawberries

1 Preheat the oven to 180°C (350°F/Gas 4) and line three 20-cm loose-bottomed cake tins. If you have only two tins you can bake two cakes first, remove from their tins to cool on a wire rack and use one of the tins again to bake the third cake.

2 Whisk the butter and sugar with the vanilla seeds or vanilla extract for about 3 minutes, or until the mixture is pale and fluffy. Add the eggs and whisk again until the mixture increases in volume.

3 Sift the flour and baking powder into the mixture and then gently fold in with a large metal spoon. Fold in the milk.

4 Scrape into the prepared tins, level the tops with a palette knife and bake in the preheated oven for 20–25 minutes. Leave to cool in their tins for at least 10 minutes before turning out on to a wire rack to cool.

5 Make the filling. Cream the butter with the vanilla extract until really soft in an electric mixer fitted with a paddle attachment. Beat for at least 3–4 minutes until pale and very creamy. Add the icing sugar, a third at a time, beating well after each addition.

6 Put half the strawberries in a food processor and blend until you have a purée; alternatively use a hand-held blender. Add just over half the strawberry purée to the filling (about 8 tablespoons) and beat again until creamy and well blended. Finely slice the remaining strawberries.

7 Make the icing by mixing together the icing sugar and 5–6 teaspoons of the remaining strawberry purée until you have a smooth icing.

8 When the cakes are completely cool, spread the first cake with a layer of the strawberry filling, a layer of finely sliced strawberries and a drizzle of remaining strawberry purée.

9 Lay the second cake on top and repeat with the remaining filling, sliced strawberries and strawberry purée. Carefully place the third cake on top.

10 Use the strawberry icing to cover the top of the cake and then decorate with edible flowers, rose petals and strawberries. This looks heavenly with tall fine taper candles for a summer birthday or party.

Miranda's variations

Prepare the cake mixture as opposite but halving the quantities. Spoon the mixture into pretty cupcake cases and bake for about 15 minutes. Decorate each cupcake with a swirl of strawberry buttercream, a drizzle of strawberry purée and a small strawberry – alpine strawberries are wonderful for this if you are lucky enough to have some in your garden. Alternatively, decorate with edible flowers.

For an alternative version of this cake, replace the strawberry buttercream with 300 ml whipped cream, whisked together with 100 g icing sugar, 1 teaspoon vanilla extract and 50 g of roughly crushed strawberries.

ELEANOR'S FLOWER FAIRY CAKES

This is the cupcake recipe I use the most, whether for tea parties, weddings, or christenings – the joy is that it can be adapted to any party theme. These flower fairy cakes are decorated with swirls of palest pink vanilla buttercream and a scattering of flower decorations and fairy dust (edible glitter or dust). The quantities given here are for quite a large number but you can easily halve it to make fewer cakes.

MAKES ABOUT 36	MAKING TIME	BAKING TIME
	20 minutes, plus decorating	15 minutes

500 g unsalted butter, softened

500 g caster sugar

1 vanilla pod, slit lengthways and seeds removed

8 large eggs, lightly beaten

2 tsp vanilla extract

500 g self-raising flour

150 ml semi-skimmed milk

For the vanilla buttercream

250 g unsalted butter, softened

80 ml semi-skimmed milk

2–3 tsp vanilla extract

800 g icing sugar, sifted

pink food colouring paste (see Miranda's Note overleaf)

sugar decorations (flowers, leaves, butterfly wings, acorns, tiny shoes etc.)

1 Preheat the oven to 180°C (350°F/Gas 4) and line an assortment of cupcake, muffin and fairy cake tins with paper cases.

2 Cream together the softened butter, caster sugar and vanilla seeds in a large bowl or in an electric mixer. Whisk until creamy and fluffy.

3 Add the eggs approximately one at a time to the butter and sugar, whisking well after each addition. Once all the egg has been whisked in and the mix is airy and well combined, add the vanilla extract.

4 Sift the flour into a bowl and then again as you add it to the mix. Sift in a little at a time and very gently fold in with a metal spoon. Once all the flour is completely combined gently fold in the milk, a little at a time.

5 Spoon into the paper cases, filling each one about half full, and gently smooth the tops. Bake in the preheated oven for about 15 minutes or until springy to the touch. Cool on a wire rack while you prepare the buttercream.

6 Beat together the softened butter, milk, vanilla and about half of the icing sugar until very smooth and creamy – you can do this by hand or with an electric mixer. Gradually add the remaining icing sugar, beating well to combine. Add a little more milk if the mixture is too stiff.

Recipe continues overleaf

7 Using a cocktail stick, add a few spots of pink colour paste to the buttercream and mix well to combine. Only add a tiny amount of colouring at a time.

8 Once the cakes are completely cool, use a palette knife to swirl buttercream on top of each cake. You could also fill a piping bag fitted with a 1M piping nozzle with the icing. Starting in the middle of the cake, pipe a swirl of icing on top of the cake – it should look like a rose. Add sugar decorations, creating different designs on each cake.

NOTES

If you don't have (or can't find) food colouring paste, use a few drops of strained fruit spread (such as Dalfour) – strawberry and blueberry will create good colours.

COCONUT AND RASPBERRY FRIANDS

These delicate little French coconut cakes are baked with a fresh raspberry in the middle. Effortless to make and meltingly good to eat – serve straight from the oven, elegantly dusted with icing sugar.

MAKES ABOUT 24	MAKING TIME	BAKING TIME
	20 minutes	25–30 minutes

5 large egg whites

150 g unsalted butter, melted, plus extra for greasing

185 g icing sugar

85 g desiccated coconut

50 g plain flour

150 g raspberries

1 Preheat the oven to 180°C (350°F/Gas 4). Lightly grease two 12-hole cupcake trays or mini muffin tins by spraying with oil or brushing with melted butter.

2 Gently whisk the egg whites just until frothy and combined; I do this by hand with a balloon whisk.

3 Add the melted butter, icing sugar, coconut and flour and mix well with a metal spoon.

4 Spoon (or pour, if easier) the mixture into each hole, filling each one no more than two-thirds full.

5 Press a raspberry into the top of each friand – you can leave some as plain coconut if you prefer. Bake in the preheated oven for about 25–30 minutes until springy to the touch. Use a palette knife to gently pop them out of their tins and on to a wire rack to cool when they come out of the oven.

PINK SUGAR-ICED CAKE WITH CANDLES

The kind of birthday cake found in children's storybooks; this one is inspired by the pink sugar-iced cake in *Winnie the Pooh*. Tall, slender taper candles look stunning and add dramatic height to the cake.

SERVES 8	MAKING TIME	BAKING TIME
	30 minutes	25–30 minutes

4 large eggs
400 g caster sugar
400 g plain flour
4 tsp baking powder
150 g unsalted butter
200 ml semi-skimmed milk
2 tsp vanilla extract
strawberry jam, for the filling

For the pink icing
300 g icing sugar
a few drops of pink food colouring
3 tablespoons water

1 Preheat the oven to 180°C (350°F/Gas 4). Lightly oil two 20-cm round sandwich tins and then lightly dust with flour, or line with non-stick baking paper or cake tin liners.

2 Using a hand-held mixer or the whisk attachment in an electric mixer, whisk together the eggs and sugar for about 5 minutes, or until pale and fluffy. Reduce the speed and gradually add the flour and baking powder. Alternatively fold in with a metal spoon.

3 Melt the butter in a jug in the microwave for about 30 seconds, or warm in a small pan. Add the milk and vanilla extract to the jug or pan, then add to the cake mixture and stir until well combined.

4 Spoon into the prepared tins and bake in the preheated oven for 25–30 minutes until the cakes are golden and springy to the touch. Allow to cool in the tin and then turn out on to a wire rack. Once they are completely cool, sandwich together with the jam.

5 Sift the icing sugar then mix together with a few drops of pink colour paste and the 3 tablespoons of water to make a runny icing. Spread on top of the cake, encouraging it to run down the sides a little. Add pretty candles and enjoy!

WALNUT AND BROWN BREAD ALMOST-ICE CREAM CAKE

This cake was inspired by the delicious flavours in old-fashioned homemade brown bread ice cream. Caramelised brown breadcrumbs are blended with toasted walnuts to make a heavenly flavoured cake, sandwiched with vanilla cream, and speckled with toffee titbits.

SERVES AT LEAST 8	MAKING TIME	BAKING TIME
	30 minutes	35–40 minutes

6 large eggs, separated

200 g caster sugar

icing sugar, for dusting

6 tbsp dulce de leche
(I use Nestlé Carnation Caramel),
warmed, for drizzling

For the caramelised breadcrumbs

100 g wholemeal brown bread,
crumbled into pieces

200 g light muscovado sugar

200 g toasted walnuts

For the filling

100 g wholemeal brown bread,
crumbled into pieces

200 g light muscovado sugar

300 ml double cream

1 vanilla pod, slit lengthways and
seeds removed

1 Preheat the oven to 180°C (350°F/Gas 4) and line two 18 cm round loose-bottomed cake tins or; alternatively use a cake tin liner.

2 Put the bread, light muscovado sugar and walnuts for the caramelised breadcrumbs on a baking sheet and mix a little to combine.

3 Put the bread and light muscovado sugar for the filling on another baking sheet and again, mix a little to combine. Place both baking trays in the preheated oven for about 10 minutes; check after 5 minutes and shuffle the crumbs around a little. The crumbs should be toffee-coloured and well caramelised – keep an eye on them as you don't want a burnt taste.

4 Put the tray of caramelised crumbs without the walnuts to one side for use in the filling.

5 To make the cake, whisk the egg yolks and caster sugar in an electric mixer until thick, pale and voluminous – this will take about 5 minutes.

6 Whizz the caramelised crumbs (with walnuts) in a food processor until ground to a breadcrumb texture – not too fine. Fold into the egg and sugar mixture with a metal spoon.

7 Whisk the egg whites until they form stiff peaks, in an electric mixer fitted with a whisk attachment or with a hand-held electric whisk. Fold into the cake mixture. Spoon into the prepared tins and bake in the preheated oven for about 35–40 minutes until springy and coming away from the sides of the tin. Leave to cool in the tin then turn out on to a rack.

Recipe continues overleaf

8 While the cake is in the oven, finish making the filling. Whisk the cream with the vanilla seeds until thick. Fold in the reserved caramelised crumbs and put in a bowl in the fridge until you are ready to put the cake together. Do not fill the cake until just before you are ready to serve it. Dust the top with icing sugar and drizzle with the warmed caramel sauce.

Miranda's variation

Try replacing the whipped cream with a tub of good-quality vanilla ice cream – leave to soften at room temperature a little before mixing in the caramelised breadcrumbs. Use this to sandwich the two cakes together and serve immediately.

RASPBERRY, PASSION FRUIT AND ALMOND CAKE

A flourless (and therefore gluten free) almond cake, meringue-like in its lightness, is layered with fresh, gently squashed raspberries and passion fruit and adorned with vanilla-infused mascarpone cream.

SERVES 10	MAKING TIME	BAKING TIME
	30 minutes	35 minutes

9 large eggs, separated

375 g caster sugar

525 g ground almonds

2½ tsp gluten-free baking powder

icing sugar, for dusting

For the filling

250 g mascarpone

200 ml fromage frais

1 tsp caster sugar

1 tsp vanilla extract

6 passion fruit

150 g fresh raspberries

Miranda's variation

This recipe can be adapted to make a delicious gluten-free chocolate cake by replacing 50 g ground almonds with 50 g gluten-free cocoa powder. Fill with chocolate ganache (see page 26).

1 Preheat the oven to 180°C (350°F/Gas 4) and line two 23-cm loose-bottomed round cake tins with non-stick baking paper.

2 Whisk the egg whites in a clean bowl until they form stiff peaks. In a separate bowl (or in the mixer with the whisk attachment) whisk together the egg yolks and sugar until pale and fluffy – about 5 minutes at high speed is about right. Gently fold in the whisked egg whites with a large metal spoon.

3 Fold in the ground almonds and baking powder, a third at a time, using the same metal spoon. Spoon into the prepared tins and bake in the preheated oven for 35 minutes, or until springy to the touch and coming away from the sides of the tin slightly. Leave to cool in the tin for about 10 minutes before carefully running a palette knife around the edge and turning out on to a wire rack to cool completely.

4 Make the filling. Use a balloon whisk to whisk together the mascarpone, fromage frais, caster sugar and vanilla extract. Remove the pulp and seeds from 3 passion fruit and stir into the filling.

5 Put the pulp and seeds from the 3 remaining passion fruit in a bowl with the raspberries and gently crush together.

6 Put one of the cakes on a cake stand, top with a layer of the raspberry and passion fruit mixture then a thick layer of the mascarpone cream. Put the other cake on top.

7 Cut a heart out of the centre of a folded piece of paper and place on top of the cake. Alternatively cut small flowers out of a piece of paper or position a doily on top of the cake. Dust generously with icing sugar then lift the paper away carefully.

NO-BAKE CAKES

POPCORN, CRANBERRY AND PISTACHIO PIECES

Dark chocolate and honey-enrobed popcorn with cranberries, pistachio nuts and sultanas. An almost virtuous rocky road?

MAKES AT LEAST 15 PIECES

MAKING TIME
10 minutes

300 g good-quality chocolate
    (70% cocoa solids)

50 g clear honey

100 g unsalted butter

75 g popcorn

75 g dried cranberries

100 g sultanas

150 g pistachio nuts

50 g toasted flaked
    almonds (optional)

1 Line a 20 x 30 cm tray bake tin with non-stick baking paper. Melt the chocolate, honey and butter in a bowl over a pan of simmering water; alternatively melt in the microwave in short bursts.

2 Stir in the popcorn, cranberries, sultanas and two-thirds of the pistachios and mix well to combine.

3 Tip the mixture into the lined tin and spread out. Sprinkle the remaining pistachios and the toasted flaked almonds, if using, on top and then place in the fridge to set. Slice into fingers or squares before serving.

CHOCOLATE AMARETTI MOUSSE CAKE

Amaretti biscuits are soaked in Cointreau, and then layered with a rich, dark chocolate mousse to make an indulgent and unforgettable pudding.

SERVES 8

MAKING TIME
20 minutes

225 g amaretti biscuits, roughly crushed

85 ml of Cointreau

450 g plain chocolate (70% cocoa solids)

110 g unsalted butter

2 large egg yolks

568 ml double cream

icing sugar, to dust

1 Line a 20-cm round (or heart-shaped, if you have one) springform cake tin with non-stick baking paper.

2 Roughly crush the amaretti biscuits, put them in a bowl and pour over the Cointreau.

3 Melt the chocolate in a bowl over a pan of simmering water. Remove from the heat and beat in the butter and egg yolks.

4 Whip the cream to soft peaks, in a mixer, using an electric hand-held whisk or in a separate bowl. Fold the cream into the chocolate mixture.

5 Spread a layer of chocolate mousse in the base of the tin (about one-third). Spoon about half the soaked amaretti on top and then follow with another layer of chocolate mousse, then the remaining amaretti biscuits. Finish with the remaining chocolate mousse and use a palette knife to smooth the top.

6 Chill in the fridge for a couple of hours then carefully remove from the tin (I find this easiest to serve upside down).

7 Fold a piece of paper in half then cut a heart shape out of the middle. Lay the paper over the top of the cake and dust with icing sugar. Carefully remove the paper to reveal a pretty icing sugar heart.

TIN ROOF TRAY

When I was growing up, one of my friend's mothers was famous for her tin roof pie. This American favourite of chewy caramel, salted peanuts and chocolate is often topped with ice cream. My quick version is sliced into bars, but it would also make a great pudding with ice cream on the side!

**MAKES AT LEAST
15 SLICES**

MAKING TIME
20 minutes

125 g peanut butter

80 ml golden syrup

80 ml honey

45 g cocoa powder

55 g light brown sugar

180 g marshmallows

80 g cornflakes

20 g rice crispies

For the topping

225 g plain chocolate (I use Belgian or Bournville)

4 tbsp double cream

120 g salted peanuts

icing sugar, to dust

1 Line a 20 x 30-cm tray bake tin with non-stick baking paper.

2 Put all the ingredients except the marshmallows, cornflakes and rice crispies in a pan and melt over a gentle heat.

3 Once the mixture is liquid and smooth, add the marshmallows and stir until they have melted into the chocolatey mixture.

4 Remove from the heat, stir in the cornflakes and rice crispies and press into the prepared tin.

5 To make the topping, put the chocolate in a bowl and melt carefully in the microwave in short bursts; alternatively place over a bowl of simmering water. Once the chocolate has melted, stir in the cream and mix well to combine.

6 Fold in the peanuts then spread over the top of the base. Smooth with a palette knife and chill in the fridge for a couple of hours before dredging with icing sugar and slicing into bars.

PANFORTE SALAMI

Panforte can be found across Italy. This dark chocolate, honey and nut recipe contains many of the traditional ingredients, but does not require any baking. This 'salami' is lovely cut into slices and enjoyed as a treat with coffee after dinner.

**MAKES TWO SALAMIS
(EACH 20 x 4 CM)**

MAKING TIME
20 minutes

200 g plain chocolate
  (I use Bournville)

80 g unsalted butter

200 g mixed nuts (choose
  from pine nuts, hazelnuts,
  almonds, pistachios)

100 g dried fruit (choose
  from apricots, dates,
  cranberries, candied peel)

200 g digestive biscuits,
  roughly crushed

30 ml clear honey

50 ml Vin Santo or other
  dessert wine or port

100 g icing sugar

½ tsp salt

2 large egg yolks

1 tsp vanilla extract

icing sugar, for dusting and rolling

1 Put the chocolate and butter in a bowl over a pan of simmering water to melt.

2 Put the nuts, dried fruits and crushed biscuits into a bowl with the honey and about half of the Vin Santo.

3 Once the chocolate is melted, add the icing sugar, salt, egg yolks, vanilla and remaining Vin Santo. Stir over the heat for about 4 minutes to ensure the eggs are cooked through.

4 Remove from the heat and add the fruit, nut and biscuit mixture. Stir well to combine then leave to cool and firm up a little.

5 Put two pieces of cling film on the worktop to make a double layer. Spoon half the mixture in a thick line in the middle – no longer than 20 cm long. On another double layer of clingfilm, make another log with the remaining mixture. Use the cling film to roll them into a sausage shape. Place on a flat board and chill in the fridge for at least 2 hours.

6 To serve, unwrap from the cling film and then roll in the icing sugar to dust completely. Cut into slices to serve.

NOTE
To give this to someone as a present, wrap like a salami in baking paper and tie the ends with string.

CHEWY CARAMEL CRISPIES

Sweet and sticky and swathed in melted caramel and marshmallow pieces, these crispies are dangerously moreish!

MAKES ABOUT 15 PIECES

MAKING TIME
15 minutes

125 g unsalted butter
200 g toffees
200 g mini marshmallows
200 g rice crispies
200 g plain or milk chocolate

1 Line a 20 x 30-cm tray bake tin with non-stick baking paper.

2 Put the butter and toffees in a large pan and melt over a gentle heat. Add the marshmallows and stir until they have melted.

3 Mix in the rice crispies and stir to evenly cover. Tip into the prepared tin and press down.

4 Carefully melt the chocolate in a microwave on high for about 1 minute, stir then return to the microwave for another minute or until completely melted and smooth. Alternatively, melt the chocolate in a heatproof bowl over a pan of barely simmering water.

5 Spread the melted chocolate over the top of the flattened rice-crispie mixture.

6 Chill in the fridge for at least 1 hour before removing from the tin and slicing into squares or bars.

CARAMELISED NUT AND SHORTBREAD CRUNCH

Caramelised almonds, toasted hazelnuts and buttery crisp shortbread pieces are smothered in milk chocolate. Simply delicious.

MAKES ABOUT 15 PIECES

MAKING TIME
15 minutes

225 g almonds, roughly chopped

150 g hazelnuts

150 g caster sugar

2 tbsp water

350 g good-quality milk chocolate

125 g unsalted butter

2 tbsp golden syrup

150 g shortbread, broken into 1-cm chunks

150 g good-quality plain chocolate (70% cocoa solids), melted

1 Line a 20-cm round loose-bottomed cake tin with non-stick baking paper. Place a sheet of baking paper on a baking sheet (for the nuts to cool on).

2 Put the almonds and hazelnuts in a large pan with the caster sugar and water and place over a low heat. Stir until the sugar has dissolved and starts to bubble; keep stirring until the nuts are coated in the golden caramel. Tip on to the prepared baking sheet and leave to cool. Once cold and hard, chop roughly into pieces.

3 Melt the 350 g of milk chocolate, butter and syrup in a bowl over a pan of simmering water. Stir in the broken shortbread and chopped caramelised nuts.

4 Spoon the mixture into the prepared tin and spread to cover the base.

5 Drizzle the mixture with the melted plain chocolate. Allow to cool completely before cutting into slices.

Miranda's variation

For a salted caramel version, sprinkle the nuts with 1 teaspoon of sea salt just after you tip them on to the baking sheet to cool.

SAVOURY
CAKES

PIZZA CAKE

The speediest cheese and olive oil cake, smothered with all your favourite pizza ingredients!

SERVES 4 (MORE IF IT'S FOR CHILDREN)	MAKING TIME 15 minutes	BAKING TIME 30–35 minutes

3 large eggs

110 ml olive oil

75 ml semi-skimmed milk

40 g full-fat cream cheese

200 g self-raising flour

1 tsp baking powder

85 g Cheddar, coarsely grated

3 tbsp sun-dried tomato paste

125 g mozzarella, roughly torn

handful of olives (optional)

ham (optional – you could use other toppings here as well)

2–3 tomatoes, sliced

a few fresh basil leaves or 1 tsp dried basil

salt and freshly ground black pepper

1 Preheat the oven to 180°C (350°F/Gas 4) and line a shallow 20 x 30-cm tray bake tin with non-stick baking paper.

2 Whisk the eggs in an electric mixer at high speed for 2 minutes, then whisk in the oil, milk and cream cheese.

3 Use a metal spoon to fold in the flour, baking powder and grated cheese, reserving a little of the cheese for the topping.

4 Scrape the mixture into the prepared tin. Spread the sun-dried tomato paste over the top then top with the mozzarella and the olives, if using, and scatter over any additional toppings and the sliced tomatoes.

5 Sprinkle over the fresh or dried basil and season with salt and pepper. Bake on the top shelf of the preheated oven for 30–35 minutes until the cheese is golden and bubbling and a skewer inserted into the cake base comes out clean.

Miranda's variation

Try topping with ricottta, wild mushrooms and a sprinkling of thyme leaves instead.

CHEDDAR SCONES

Cheesy, very comforting and so incredibly simple to make.

MAKES 12	MAKING TIME	BAKING TIME
	10 minutes	15 minutes

450 g self-raising flour

1 tsp salt

2 tsp baking powder

110 g chilled unsalted butter, diced

200 g strong Cheddar,
  coarsely grated

1½ tsp mustard

½ tsp cayenne pepper or paprika

1 large egg

about 250 ml semi-skimmed milk

1 Preheat the oven to 200°C (400°F/Gas 6) and line two baking sheets with non-stick baking paper.

2 Sift the flour, salt and baking powder into a bowl and rub in the butter with your fingers; alternatively whizz in a food processor.

3 Use a knife to mix in the cheese (keeping a handful aside to put on top of the scones), mustard and cayenne pepper or paprika.

4 Crack the egg into a measuring jug and add enough milk to top up the liquid to 300 ml. Beat lightly with a fork and then add this mixture to the bowl.

5 Mix to a rough dough in the bowl and then pull together with your hands and turn out on to a lightly floured surface. Gently flatten to about 4 cm thick. Use a small round cutter to cut out 12 scones – press down and pull straight out, do not twist the cutter.

6 Place the scones on the lined baking sheet, sprinkle the remaining cheese on top and bake in the preheated oven for about 15 minutes, or until golden on the top and underneath. Leave to cool on the baking sheets for a few minutes before moving to a wire rack to firm up a little.

TASTY CHEESE AND CHUTNEY MUFFINS

Perfect for picnics, these muffins are like a little parcel of a ploughman's lunch! Great to make with cheese that needs using up and any chutney you might have to hand.

MAKES 12	MAKING TIME 10 minutes	BAKING TIME 20 minutes

250 ml semi-skimmed milk

3 large eggs

400 g plain flour (or 200 g plain flour and 200 g wholemeal flour)

1½ tbsp baking powder

200 g Stilton or Cheddar, grated (keep a handful of cheese to one side to sprinkle on top before baking)

100 g walnuts or pecan nuts, roughly broken up (optional)

3 tbsp chutney or onion marmalade

½ tsp sea salt and freshly ground black pepper

1 Preheat the oven to 200°C (400°F/Gas 6) and line a 12-hole muffin tray with squares of non-stick baking paper.

2 Put the milk and eggs into a jug and beat together with a fork.

3 Put the flour and baking powder into a large mixing bowl and add salt and pepper. Stir together to combine. Add the cheese, walnuts or pecans, chutney and the egg and milk mixture. Mix well with a wooden spoon.

4 Spoon into the prepared tray, sprinkle with cheese and bake in the preheated oven for about 20 minutes, or until golden and springy to the touch. Eat while still warm.

LITTLE APPLE AND CHEESE OAT BREADS

A simple way to introduce children, or impatient bakers, to homemade bread.

MAKES 12 ROLLS	MAKING TIME	BAKING TIME
	10 minutes	20 minutes

200 g self-raising flour

2 tsp baking powder

25 g oats, plus extra for sprinkling

25 g unsalted butter, diced

2 eating apples, peeled
and coarsely grated

120 g mature Cheddar, coarsely grated

1 tsp mustard

1 large egg, lightly beaten

salt and freshly ground black pepper

1 Preheat the oven to 220°C (425°F/Gas 7) and line a baking sheet with non-stick baking paper or use a loaf tin liner.

2 Sift the flour and baking powder into a bowl and stir in the oats and some salt and pepper. Rub in the butter with your fingers; alternatively whizz together in a food processor.

3 Stir in the grated apples, cheese and mustard and then mix in the egg, keeping a teaspoonful to one side to glaze the tops.

4 Bring together with your hands and then form into 12 rough balls. Place on the lined baking sheet and then slash a deep cross in the middle of each ball of dough. Brush the tops with the remaining egg and sprinkle with a few oats.

5 Bake in the preheated oven for about 20 minutes. To check if they're done, lift one up with a palette knife and peek underneath; it should lift away cleanly and be mottled and golden on the bottom. Transfer to a wire rack to cool.

STILTON, PEAR AND WALNUT LOAF

This savoury loaf cake is packed with a winning medley of Stilton, pear and walnut. It is best eaten warm with green salad and makes a delicious lunch or starter.

MAKES ONE 2-LB LOAF	MAKING TIME	BAKING TIME
	10 minutes	30–35 minutes

3 large eggs

110 ml olive oil

75 ml semi-skimmed milk

40 g full-fat cream cheese

200 g self-raising flour

1 tsp baking powder

110 g Stilton, roughly chopped

80 g walnuts, roughly chopped

2 pears (about 100 g), peeled, cored and roughly chopped

salt and freshly ground black pepper

1 Preheat the oven to 180°C (350°F/Gas 4) and line a 2-lb loaf tin with non-stick baking paper or use a loaf tin liner.

2 Whisk the eggs in an electric mixer at high speed for about 2 minutes then whisk in the oil, milk and cream cheese.

3 Use a metal spoon to fold in the flour and baking powder, then fold in the Stilton and walnuts, reserving a little of each to sprinkle over the top of the loaf. Finally stir in the chopped pears.

4 Scrape the mixture into the prepared tin. Sprinkle the reserved cheese and walnuts on top and bake on a low shelf in the preheated oven for 30–35 minutes until springy to the touch. Allow to cool in the tin for about 5 minutes. This is best eaten while still warm.

HONEY BASTABLE CAKE (IRISH SODA BREAD)

Traditionally soda bread would have been baked in a bastable oven, a cast-iron pot with a concave lid that is covered with smouldering turf. There are still parts of Ireland that call soda bread 'bastable cake' for this reason. The addition of oats and honey makes the loaf even more nourishing and satisfying. My friend Mary, from Ireland, still makes soda bread every day for her family and is known to make spares and bring them when she calls by!

MAKES ONE 2-LB LOAF	MAKING TIME	BAKING TIME
	10 minutes	40–45 minutes

350 g plain flour

150 g wholemeal plain flour

1 tsp salt

2 tsp bicarbonate of soda

100 g oats (keep a handful to sprinkle on top)

2 tbsp honey, warmed

400 ml buttermilk or natural (live) yoghurt

1 Preheat the oven to 200°C (400°F/Gas 6) and oil and flour a 2-lb loaf tin, or use a loaf tin liner.

2 Put all the dry ingredients into a large mixing bowl and stir to combine. Make a well in the centre.

3 Stir the warm honey into the buttermilk or yoghurt and add to the dry ingredients. Mix with a wooden spoon and then bring together with your hands.

4 Tip on to a lightly floured surface and knead gently – it shouldn't need more than about 1 minute to form a soft dough. Pop into the loaf tin and sprinkle the remaining oats on top. Bake in the preheated oven for 40–45 minutes, or until golden brown on top and coming away from the sides of the tin.

5 Leave to cool completely in the tin; traditionally the loaves would have been left for about 4 hours before eating.

SWEET POTATO, ROASTED PEPPER AND CHORIZO LOAF

This is unbelievably tasty, as well as being quick and easy to make. It's delicious eaten warm with soup or strong cheese and chutney, and is great, too, as an unusual bread with a starter or main course. You can also make a delicious vegetarian version by simply leaving out the chorizo.

MAKES ONE 2-LB LOAF	MAKING TIME	BAKING TIME
	20 minutes	30 minutes

300 g sweet potato

80 ml olive oil (or use the oil from the peppers)

150 g chorizo, finely sliced

2 large eggs

150 g self-raising flour (or 100 g self-raising flour and 50 g wholemeal plain flour)

1 tsp bicarbonate of soda

½ tsp salt

2 tsp paprika

100g roasted peppers in oil, drained and chopped

handful of mixed seeds, for sprinkling

1 Preheat the oven to 170°C (325°F/Gas 3) and line a 2-lb loaf tin with non-stick baking paper or use a loaf tin liner.

2 Prick the skin of the sweet potatoes with a fork and then put them on a plate in the microwave and cook on high heat for about 10 minutes. Slice in half and use a metal spoon to scrape the flesh out into a bowl. Alternatively, peel, chop and cook the sweet potatoes in boiling water for about 10 minutes until soft and then drain. Mash with a fork in a large bowl.

3 Heat 1 tablespoon of the olive oil in a pan and gently fry the chorizo until crisp. Set aside.

4 Add the eggs and remaining oil to the sweet potato then stir in the dry ingredients. Add the peppers, chorizo and the spicy oil you fried it in to the mixture, reserving about 6 slices to put on top of the loaf at the end. Mix well to combine.

5 Scrape into the prepared tin and top with the reserved chorizo slices and a sprinkling of mixed seeds. Bake in the preheated oven for about 30–35 minutes or until a skewer inserted into the centre comes out clean. Leave to cool in the tin.

PYJAMA MUFFINS

A 'full English' baked in a muffin. Great fun if you have friends to stay or coming for brunch. Fry one cooked breakfast and, as if by magic, turn it into breakfast for twelve! You can add any breakfast ingredients you like, omitting or adding ingredients to suit your guests.

MAKES 12	MAKING TIME	BAKING TIME
	15 minutes	20 minutes

250 ml semi-skimmed milk

4 large eggs

150 g unsalted butter, melted

500 g self-raising flour

2 tsp baking powder

½ tsp sea salt

freshly ground black pepper

For the breakfast filling

4 chipolatas

4 rindless smoked bacon rashers

handful of mushrooms, sliced (optional)

handful of cherry tomatoes, halved

2 tbsp baked beans

tomato ketchup

1 Preheat the oven to 200°C (400°F/Gas 6) and line a 12-hole muffin tray with cake cases.

2 Fry the breakfast filling ingredients (except the baked beans and ketchup) in one pan and then put to one side to cool a little. Snip the chipolatas and bacon rashers into smaller pieces (or use leftovers!).

3 Put the milk and eggs into a large jug and beat together with a fork, then add the melted butter.

4 Put the flour, baking powder, salt and pepper into a large mixing bowl. Stir to combine. Add the egg, milk and butter mixture and mix well with a wooden spoon.

5 Mix all the breakfast ingredients except the ketchup and baked beans into the mixture. If you are catering for vegetarians, spoon some of the mixture into another bowl and stir the vegetarian breakfast ingredients in separately. Stir well to combine.

6 Spoon into the prepared muffin tray, filling each one half full. Add some ketchup or a spoonful of baked beans on to the mixture then top up with more mixture on top to almost fill the muffin hole. Bake in the preheated oven for 20 minutes or until pale golden on top. Serve immediately.

RÖSTI CAKE

Crammed full of melting Swiss cheese, potatoes and smoked bacon, this rösti cake will transport you to lunch at an Alpine café on the slopes. Far quicker and easier to make than a quiche or pie, this cake is quirky and tasty.

SERVES 4–6 (DEPENDING ON APPETITE!)	MAKING TIME 20 minutes	BAKING TIME 35 minutes

25 g breadcrumbs (about 1 slice of bread)

3 large baking potatoes (about 1 kg), alternatively use the same quantity of leftover mashed potato

100 ml olive oil

200 g chopped pancetta, smoked bacon or smoked ham

1 garlic clove, crushed

150 ml semi-skimmed milk

4 large eggs

75 g flour

2 tsp baking powder

40 g grated Parmesan

100 g grated Gruyère, plus 1 tbsp for sprinkling

salt and freshly ground black pepper

1 Preheat the oven to 200°C (400°F/Gas 6). Lightly oil a 20-cm round cake tin and sprinkle some of the breadcrumbs inside – this will give a crispy crust to the cake.

2 Put the baking potatoes on a plate in the microwave and bake for about 15 minutes. Meanwhile, heat about 1 teaspoon of the oil in a pan and fry the pancetta or bacon with the crushed garlic until crisp.

3 When the potatoes are cooked, slice them in half and use a metal spoon to scrape the flesh out into a bowl; alternatively use leftover mashed potato. Add about one-third of the olive oil and one-third of the milk and mash roughly with a fork.

4 Put the eggs in a jug with the remaining milk and oil and beat with a fork to combine. Add to the mashed potato and mix well with a wooden spoon to combine. Add the garlicky pancetta, flour, baking powder, grated cheeses and some salt and pepper and mix in well.

5 Tip the mixture into the prepared cake tin and sprinkle the remaining breadcrumbs and Gruyère on top. Bake in the preheated oven for about 35 minutes or until golden on top and firm to the touch.

6 Remove from the oven and leave to stand in the tin for about 10 minutes before transferring to a serving plate and eating immediately.

SUN-DRIED TOMATO AND PARMESAN MUFFINS

These little muffins are soufflé-like in their cheesy lightness and are great to whip up when you have unexpected guests for lunch. They are also equally at home as a homemade starter or, in miniature form, as party nibbles.

MAKES 12

MAKING TIME
10 minutes

BAKING TIME
20 minutes

250 ml semi-skimmed milk

3 large eggs

400 g plain flour

2 tsp baking powder

4 tbsp red pesto

200 g grated Parmesan

100 g sun-dried tomatoes, roughly chopped

handful of pine nuts, for sprinkling

salt and freshly ground black pepper

1 Preheat the oven to 200°C (400°F/Gas 6) and line a 12-hole muffin tray with squares of non-stick baking paper.

2 Put the milk and eggs into a jug and beat together with a fork.

3 Put the flour and baking powder into a large mixing bowl and add salt and pepper. Stir together to combine. Add the pesto, three-quarters of the Parmesan and the sun-dried tomatoes, along with the egg and milk mixture. Mix well with a wooden spoon.

4 Spoon into the prepared tray. Sprinkle the tops with the remaining Parmesan and a few pine nuts before putting them in the preheated oven to bake for 20 minutes until golden and springy to the touch.

5 Serve straight from the oven as a delicious lunch or as a starter with rocket leaves and a balsamic glaze.

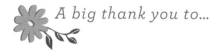 *A big thank you to...*

My mother, for a childhood filled with cake, rough snow icing and the taste of home,
and for inspiring me to always get one more thing done.

My mother-in-law, for being the curator of many family recipes and for always being
at the end of the telephone.

All our friends, who have given me ideas, tasted, tested, listened patiently while I have waxed
lyrical about all things cake (and who have been courageous enough to give honest feedback!),
and reminded me about PE kits or school trips after late nights of recipe writing
– you know who you are!

My editor, Laura, for being tirelessly patient and understanding, and to Lizzy and everyone at
Ebury and Random House for their enthusiasm and commitment to making my book a reality.

Annie, Rosie, Miranda '2' and Sarah, for being the best photo-shoot team imaginable, for their
styling, planning, forward thinking, understanding, creativity, friendship and fun, and for making
the cakes and photographs look so beautiful.

Elly and Heather, for their sound advice and welcome reassurance.

Caitlin, for playing with Henry, testing recipes and endlessly washing up!

The team at Chalon, for providing a temporary kitchen so that we could achieve my dream of
taking all of the photographs for this book at home.

Squires kitchen, for pretty decorating supplies, and Kenwood for their lovely mixers.

Lyle and all our builders, for renovating our house around me while I carried
on writing recipes and baking.

My children's friends and teachers, for eating lots of spare cake!

Index